MASTERING THE STOIC
WAY OF LIFE

ANDREAS ATHANAS

MASTERING THE STOIC WAY OF LIFE

Improve Your Mental Toughness, Self-Discipline, and Productivity with Ancient Stoic Wisdom

By Andreas Athanas

indirect, which are incurred as a result of the use of information contained within this document, including, but not limited to, — errors, omissions, or inaccuracies.

❀ Created with Vellum

INTRODUCTION

The modern era is a time of both convenience and despair, innovative technological advancements and the burgeoning wants of the classes left behind, left out by the mainstream or relegated to a sideline perspective of the world's affairs. War is widespread and terrorism has surfaced as a major component of political discourse in a time marked by the disenfranchisement of vast stretches of the human population. Political upheavals and economic uncertainty are commonplace, and throughout the world, despite the dawning of communications technologies, it has never been easier to turn a blind eye toward the suffering of the less fortunate.

Not only is the world troubled on a macrocosmic level, but these struggles have manifested themselves on an individualistic level, creating problems that confront us every day and can become almost intolerable. From the raising of children to work commutes to the dangers of poverty in an increasingly unstable economy, the modern world presents innumerable stressors that add up to a bleak and dreary world for those who seek to control their own lives.

These problems, however, are as old as mankind. Since the dawn of human reason, we have been endlessly struggling—class against class, race against race, nation against nation—in such repetitive fashion the trials of today seem like mere echoes of an age-old story.

Enter Greek philosophy.

Since the days of Socrates, philosophy has sought the betterment of man and the enlightenment of human reason in environments that preclude any sort of true advancement. From amidst the sea of despair, though, many thoughts have arisen that give mankind the ability to reckon its own position within the cosmos, to make sense of the insensible and attempt to construct valid and practicable notions of human emotion, reason, and intellect. Of these myriad schools of thought, one stands out as the predominant methodology for handling the stresses of life, whether those stresses originate in ancient Athens or twenty-first century America. This school of thought is known as Stoicism and, since its inception, has served as a bastion to the free thinker. It has drawn intellectuals from every walk of life into its fold because it relies, for its philosophical disposition, on an introspective train of thought related not to the troubles of the outside world, but the troubles of the soul.

For over 2,500 years, Stoicism has been an active player in the discourse of human rationality and has gained esteemed philosophers, such as Marcus Aurelius, as proponents of the theories posited therein. The beauty of this philosophy lies in its simplicity. It seeks only to aid humankind in the navigation of emotional distress and holds the position that emotional duress is predominantly caused by our own understanding—or lack thereof—of the sources of such duress.

In the modern age, Stoicism has resurfaced as the primary basis of successful schools of psychological thought and has adapted to fit the rigors of modern society and the needs of the people it seeks to address. Times have obviously changed since the

original Stoics walked through the marble columns
and temples of old Athens, but the philosophy that
they preached in that bygone era has still remained a
central focus of human advancement in both the
philosophical and psychological doctrines.

What to make of this seemingly timeless quality
of an ancient philosophy? Maybe it speaks to the
truth of the Stoic method and stands as implicit
evidence that the man who first formulated the
tenets of Stoic thought might have been onto something that tapped into the very nature of the human
mind. The manner in which this philosophy has
adapted to a variety of social settings and political
atmospheres also indicates the universality of Zeno's
message. Much of the Stoic mindset has been
adopted and adapted to so many different areas of
human life and culture, but one aspect that has
remained the same is its central focus on improvement of the individual over improvement of society,
and it has always prescribed some form of meditative introspection as the means to achieve that end.
That the common vein of all Stoicism's incarnations
would be this inward focus, this act of self-inspec-
tion, taps into what all branches of philosophy are
about. Given this, we can say that Zeno and the
Stoics were not only the founders of a movement of

their own but did so through further developing that study of wisdom and that they are deserving of far more credit than they are typically awarded.

The modern philosophical discourse of our intellectual elite has once again come full circle and retouched upon the issues that the original Stoics first came to confront. Now, rather than existing as a philosophy, it remains "behind the scenes", working as an active agent by informing psychological discourse and reaffirming the original tenets of the ancient philosophy. Today, many forms of psychotherapy have their roots in the old Stoic traditions. Cognitive Behavioral Therapy borrows heavily from Stoic principles and the splintering methods of psychological healing that stem from CBT, all owe something to the original teachings of Ancient Greece. Despite the changing times, Stoicism still has something to offer humanity and its frequent reincarnations throughout history point to its primacy as a method a therapeutic understanding of the human soul.

In this book, we will discuss the evolution of Stoicism as a moral and ethical philosophy and as an intellectual framework that has informed modern medicine and psychiatry. Through this study, we hope to shed light on current developments in this ancient way of life and delineate ways in which it can be implemented by citizens of the modern world. The aim of the study of Stoicism is, and always has been, self-improvement and a rational introspection related to the control of emotional responses in human beings. In a modern context, this conversation necessitates an overview of psychological paradigms that have informed our contemporary thoughts on the field of memory, emotion, and the biological apparatuses that operate within our brains to bring about what we, as conscious beings, experience as emotion.

Furthering this discussion into the realm of the practical, we will then describe the benefits of embracing a Stoic mind state, and give the reader an idea of how to go about achieving this philosophical disposition. By framing this discussion as a psychological and philosophical discourse, we will attempt to bridge the gap between the two. This allows us to achieve a common ground that is the most advantageous to both an understanding of the philosophical tenets and practical applications for those tenets as they are enacted by modern psychological study.

Zeno's Legacy

One of the most important aspects of Zeno's legacy, and one that exists as separate from the tenets of the philosophy he created, is his role in bringing elevated thought into the arena of mainstream Greek society. Through his open-door teaching style, he spread his message on the streets of Athens, not merely among its social and political elite, as previous philosophers had done before him. This focus on the people is both a requisite stipulation of the content of his philosophy as a philosophy of action and means by which he sought to enact a change in the viewpoints of the people around him. As Marcus Aurelius points out, a loaf of bread does far more good to the hungry man than a philosophical discourse about whether or not bread good or evil, indifferent or otherwise (Kamtekar 2017). By making philosophy a discussion in which layman could contribute, Zeno broke from the traditional way of doing things and created a new paradigm that would inform radical political and social discourse in the intervening centuries. His innovations to the art of thinking with a level head, sent tremors through his contemporary intellectual community that are still felt today, and his disciples throughout the ages have been, in some cases, literally deified for their thoughts and lifestyles.

In a way, Zeno is the world's first philosophical populist, and he railed against the elitism of other philosophical schools for their inability to tap into what the people of the streets cared about. Obtuse and impenetrable discourse would never do anything to cure the ills that Zeno observed in his society because they would not allow for the opinions of the uneducated. By shifting this paradigm, Zeno instills his philosophy with both staying power and vigor that the teachings of Socrates and Aristotle did not have. In this fashion, Stoicism truly is a philosophy of action. From its very inception, the history of the school of thought is laden with living principles and lessons that Zeno believed would do far more good than the roundabout discussions of the intellectual elite.

His work is remembered because he sought to have it so. His work affected the lives of so many subsequent scholars and rulers because it is in the most foundational principles of the tenets that such a philosophy should be for everyone, and that the benefits of enlightenment were not the sanctified privilege of the upper-class. By taking this stance, he created a philosophy that would speak to the poor and the slaves, the orphans and women who have no agency in society at all, much less agency over the workings of the world. This contributed to his vast number of followers and disciples that carried on his message after his death. The creation of a philosophy aimed at the betterment of everyone is a philosophy that can be followed by anyone, anywhere in the world, at any point in history. Wherever the disenchanted amass, Stoic philosophy finds an audience because the philosophy seeks to address what causes disenchantment in the first place, putting us in control of its spread and giving us the tools to combat it.

This arguably does far more for an individual than any preaching by Socrates, Plato, or Aristotle, who spent their lives discussing that which had no bearing on the population as a whole. Zeno's legacy is built on the notion of a populist philosophy that speaks to a wide swath of people and can be applied in a wide variety of circumstances to enact positive change in those who stick to its values. He is remembered, not unlike Prometheus himself, for bringing the light of wisdom down from its lofty heights and gifting it to the world in a form that was understandable, relatable, and conducive to the betterment of individual humans at the same time it was beneficial to the world as a whole.

What Zeno gave us was a schematic toward a life well-lived and this, in the final accounting of things, is the purpose of philosophy. He taught us to live properly, in accordance with nature, and in step with not the rule of law or societal norms, but of the reason that inherently makes us unique beings. This is what appealed to the Neostoic Humanists in the seventeenth century, just as much as it appealed to the ancient Greeks and Romans and modern psychologists. Laws and societal norms are not exclusively evil from the Stoic worldview, but they create a cultural system in which humanity does not get to decide for itself how it will act. This dissonance between rationality and the rule of social laws is what engenders unhappiness, in that it prevents people from pursuing rationality as a viable method for achieving happiness. This has never been truer than it is in contemporary America, where wealth is a measure of success and status is equated to happiness. Zeno, even in today's day and age, is still relevant in that his teachings remind us of the impermanence of all that our society holds dear. And, in the end, when everything is stripped away and we are left facing the void of death, Zeno reminds us that to die is the only rational end for us and that so long as we lived according to selves and our rationality, we have nothing to fear of death.

THE HISTORY OF STOICISM

*A*s a philosophy and a way of life, Stoicism predates many of the major religions of today and was first formulated in the third century BC by a Greek philosopher named Zeno of Citium (Mark, 2015). In his youth, Zeno studied under the tutelage of prominent Greek philosopher Crates of Thebes, who founded the school of thought known as Cynicism, and to understand the roots from which Stoicism grew, it is important to understand the philosophical culture and precedents common in Ancient Greece at the time.

BECAUSE ZENO STUDIED under Crates of Thebes and is considered by history to be his most successful pupil, we must delve into the teachings of Crates, though his surviving work is limited, and knowledge about his personal life is almost nonexistent. What we do know about Crates is that much of his philosophy and his love of wisdom sprang forth from a play that he saw as the rich son of a powerful family in the Greek city of Thebes. This play, *The Tragedy of Telephon*, discusses pain and loss and centers around the semi-divine son of Heracles and a mortal wound he suffered at the hands of a Greek hero, Achilles.

IN THE PLAY, Telephon is told by an oracle that nothing will soothe his pain or ease his passing, save for the blessing of the man who inflicted this pain on him, to begin with. Telephon, always thinking fast, sneaks into Achilles' camp disguised in rags and implores the stout warrior to heal the wound.

THOUGH NOTHING IS KNOWN about how or why this play affected Crates, or what about its storyline moved him to alter his life so drastically. What is known is that shortly afterward, Crates of Thebes disavowed his inheritance, his wealth and power, and his family to pursue a life of ascetic simplicity, studying philosophy in the streets of Athens and working on perfecting a life of wisdom.

MUCH OF HIS philosophy is based on the notion that material possessions are short-lived, temporal things, destined to leave this world and those who hold them momentarily. As such, Cynics held the true pursuit of wisdom as something that existed totally separate from the commonly held desires for fame and money, power and women, lucrative businesses and enterprises and the trapping of metropolitan life in what, at that time, was the seat of contemporary civilization.

CYNICS, following the cues of a long line of Greek philosophers stretching back to Socrates in the fifth century BCE, believed in values that were akin to the Buddhist teachings that were already a couple hundred years old by this point. Possessions were fleeting and not a true measure of happiness or success. The sage did not worry himself with such matters and pursued instead a "life according to nature," removing himself from public life and taking to the streets to spread the message of poverty and purity among the people who would listen.

FOR CENTURIES, this message took hold, living long after the twilight of Greek superiority and eventually spreading to the Romans, dying out temporarily as Christianity began to dominate philosophical discussions throughout the Roman Empire, only to spring back up out of hibernation every time a world culture began to grow to excessive, and engender the birth of countercultures.

FUTURE GENERATIONS WOULD BASTARDIZE the Cynic's message until it came to be perceived as we perceive it today, namely, that anything joyous and good in this world is an evil that should be shunned, but in its earliest incarnations, Ancient Greek cynicism was a philosophy that preached simplicity, virtue, and a lifestyle free from the pursuit of vainglorious endeavor.

ZENO OF CITIUM

Zeno of Citium, known today as one of the

prominent philosophers who gifted Stoic thought to the world through his scholarship, was born three hundred years before the dawning of Christianity in what is now the island of Cyprus. Before he gave himself over to philosophy and the pursuit of a virtuous life, Zeno of Citium employed himself in commerce and built for himself vast wealth by trading commodities in the Aegean sea.

ACCORDING to the stories surrounding his life, his interest in asceticism and philosophy began after he experienced a near-death encounter on the open sea, surviving a shipwreck off the coast of modern-day Israel. After the wreck, he found himself in Athens, consulting a bookseller, through whom he first encountered the philosophical writings of Xenophon, a Socratic scholar whose works are still lauded by modern academics. It was through the words of Xenophon's *Memorabilia* that Zeno became enamored with the study of virtue and life according to the laws of nature.

THOUGH LITTLE IS KNOWN about his life, it can be inferred from the surviving works of scholarship and history that surround his influential school of thought that the wreck he experienced off the coast of Phoenicia stood in his mind as an example of how meaningless a life of acquisition and trade truly was. He had just made his profits, traded his wares and extended his commercial network as a thriving businessman, but these developments were nothing in the face of catastrophic forces of nature.

THE EFFECT of this brush with death solidified in his mind and grew into one of the primary tenets of his philosophy, namely, that property and money meant nothing and did not lead to a fulfilling life. They were transitory pleasures, to borrow a phrase from Buddhist thought, and could not guarantee anyone a pleasurable, introspective life in accordance with reason and nature. Zeno believed that doing away with societal excess was the quickest and most reliable way to ensure a culture of logic and rational thought, the best method of achieving sage-like wisdom, and the only way that one could live within the bounds of natural action and reason.

. . .

THESE THOUGHTS SEEMED radical during contemporary society in the Greek city state of Athens, the seat of wisdom and scholarship for the entire known world up to that point. In this period, intellectual thought was dominated by the hedonistic and pleasure-driven ideologies of Epicurus, who believed life was too short to waste on anything but the innumerable splendors that the sensory world had to offer the discerning palate.

TO PUT the two philosophies in contrast, Epicureans believed in four maxims that informed their thought and the patterning of their lives as they tried to live in accordance with the teachings of Epicurus. These four maxims, taken at a glance, hold as fact the absence of a divine presence or afterlife, and that the primary evils of life were to endure suffering and want. The Greek philosopher hoped to inspire his followers to forego their fear of death, their desires for what might come in an afterlife never promised, and rather enjoy the ephemeral, brief moment they had to live on this planet.

. . .

It is easy to see how this stands in stark relief to the teachings of Zeno and his Stoics, who disregarded personal possession, sought no fame or fortune, and wanted only to live a peaceful life of contemplation. To Zeno and the Stoics, the pursuit of one pleasure only led to the pursuit of another, and another after that, and still more to follow those, ad infinitum. These overlapping desires caused jealousy and crime, and led humanity down a road that ended only with the destruction of harmony between kin and friend. These passions, as Zeno described them, were the yoke that held humankind down in the gutter and only by freeing oneself from such a bond could man achieve his natural state as a rational, thinking individual existing side by side with the rest of the world. By pursuing vainglory, humans only muddied the metaphorical waters of rationality and created for themselves a tomb within which the ideals of intellectual pursuit would die.

When Zeno arrived in Athens, fresh out of his shipwreck and feeling renewed in a life that had almost been taken from him, he began writing and his discourses covered a vast array of topics generally discussed by philosophers of the time. One of his works that still survive today, entitled *Republic*, (not to be confused with Plato's groundbreaking work of the same name) followed the construction of a perfect society with no social ranking, no law or crime, and complete equality among both sexes and races of man. Such a society, posits the text, is only possible in a world bereft of passion, where men and women can pursue the natural order unfettered by cosmopolitan principles and leanings, where possessions inspired no covetousness, and where no social ladder existed for climbing.

THOUGH IT DID NOT MAKE NEARLY AS big of a mark on subsequent philosophy as Plato's work, it did inform much of what Crates, his tutor, would go on to preach in years following Zeno's demise.

ZENO'S untimely death is shrouded in mystery and modern academia is still unsure about how he eventually passed away. It is known that he committed suicide through strangulation, and the story surrounding the rash actions of a man who gave his entire life to the pursuit of rationality holds that the accident—he tripped down a step after teaching in

Athens—struck Zeno as an omen, as a prophecy of sorts, and stood to remind him that his time on earth had come to an end and that to go on any longer would be to yearn for a time of primacy that he knew from the beginning was not meant to last.

IN THIS WAY, Zeno exited the world of man, leaving not a modest footprint in his wake, but an entire school of thought that would be carried on like the Promethean torch from one scholar to the next, alternately subsiding into the darkness of forgotten history and emerging to stir the minds of another generation of youth. His work was carried on by his followers and became a major component in the worldview of the early Roman Empire, earning such famed supporters as Marcus Aurelius and esteemed thinker Seneca the Younger.

STOICISM AND CHRISTIANITY

The relationship between Stoicism and the later doctrines of Christianity has been a strange and troubled relationship. Though both philosophies employ some of the same metaphysical and ethical ideals, the rivalling powers of both schools of thought came into conflict numerous times through the ages. Both philosophies accept the inherent nature of the world as a rational, divinely providential place with humanity occupying a privileged and central role within its functioning. But in regard to the divinity of the universe, the two schools of thought differ in their interpretation. Whereas Christianity advocates for a divine source of life that exists as separate from the masses of humanity, Stoics held the belief that the divinity of the universe lies both within and without.

AN INHERENT PRINCIPLE of the teachings of the stoa holds that humanity has the providential obligation to act only on reason because reason is unique to mankind and represents a gift from the universal beings' beneficence. This is in direct contrast to the Christian notions of divinity. Despite these differences, however, the congruences that do exist between the two modes of thought are indicative of a communication of ideas that transpired during the periods of Christianity's evolution and solidification as a concrete philosophy.

. . .

IT IS KNOWN that the prominent Roman emperor and Stoic scholar, Marcus Aurelius, enacted widespread persecution of the fledgling religion during his reign in the second century AD. This is despite the fact that many of the original Christian apostles of the Biblical era preached philosophies and ways of life congruent with Zeno's teachings. St. Paul of Tarsus is believed to have been educated in the Stoic way during his youth in the Hellenistic world, and though the debate still rages about the extent to which these teachings influenced his Christianity, it can be hard to imagine that they would have made no impression at all on the Christian apostle (Grant, 1915). When comparing the teachings of Paul with the philosophies of Stoicism, they seem to be opposite one another, it is known that Paul wrote in Greek, spoke Greek, and was raised under the framework of Greek philosophical inflections of the time, which were indelibly dominated by the ideals of the stoa.

EVEN IF HIS ideas run contrary to the stoic teachings, that they exist as a reaction to the predominant mode of thought contemporary to St. Paul is indicative of the manner in which Christianity and

Stoicism have intertwined over the years. Some of the earliest Christian scholars also operated under Greek educational forms, and the juxtaposition of these two philosophies existing side by side one another and competing for the minds of the world's populace is emblematic of their relationship during the infancy of philosophy.

MOVING FORWARD, Christianity and Stoicism were brought closer together through the writing of humanist European scholars of the late renaissance who sought to use the teachings of Stoicism to explain the tragedies of the early modern period of European history.

JUSTUS LIPSIUS, in this time, further used Christian thought to analyze Stoic doctrine by attempting to apply the Stoic notion of the world's indifference toward man to a discussion about the nature of divine punishment. For Lipsius and other revivalist Stoic scholars, the uncaring world that Zeno describes is a symptom of divine providence. This merger of philosophy is an example of the interactions between these two schools of thought.

.   .   .

DESPITE THEIR DIFFERENCES and the tension between the two, no one can doubt that they existed contemporaneously, and as two dominating world views vying for followers, must have been in intellectual contact with one another.

STOICISM THROUGH THE AGES

ollowing the death of Zeno, Stoicism emerged as a primary philosophy practiced first by the Greeks contemporary to Alexander the Great, and subsequently by the Roman empire and various thinkers to the west of the Hellenistic homeland. From slaves to senators, emperors and early Christians, the ideals of Stoicism and the belief in rational thought's supremacy provided a counterbalance for intellectuals in a time where social change swept the entire known world and the commonly asserted customs and beliefs of the Roman republic gave way to the less predictable whims of a host of Roman emperors.

. . .

LEARNED LEADERS OF THE WORLD, such as Marcus Aurelius, embraced the moral stance first proposed by Zeno, and mad rulers like Nero persecuted its practice and drove it away from the common ground of accepted intellectual thought during his reign.

REGARDLESS OF HOW Stoicism was viewed by the early Roman empire, one thing remains clear: the school of thought did not die on the marble steps of ancient Athens with its progenitor. Whether underground or in the light of day, scholars continued to preach temperance, virtue, and respect for the supremacy of human logic in the natural order of the world that seemed so tumultuous in the time of Christ and the Roman land acquisitions of the first century AD.

IN THIS CHAPTER, we will delve into the lives of the proponents of Stoicism, and unpack the manner in which their intellectual debates and theories helped to shape the ideologies that would become central to western thought for the remainder of antiquity.

From the freed slave Epictetus to the lofty heights of Marcus Aurelius' throne in Rome, the spread and survival of Stoicism speaks to its adaptability and the rigor with which its adherents pursue their love of virtue in accordance with nature.

Epictetus

Born into slavery during the reign of Nero, Epictetus is a historical figure and early disseminator of the original Stoic thought who remains shrouded in mystery. Much of what we know about him today is based on vagaries and incomplete records.

WHAT WE DO KNOW, or can assume with a good degree of certainty, is that Epictetus was born in modern-day Turkey and spent most of his early life as a slave owned by wealthy freedman who earned himself great power and prominence as a secretary for Nero. He walked with a limp, and though many stories circulate about his leg being intentionally broken by his master with an aim to permanently cripple the child, it is equally as possible that he was

17

born with a birth defect that prevented him from walking properly.

HE WAS KNOWN to be a powerful orator and earned great respect after earning his freedom in the years following Nero's demise as a skilled debater and rhetorician. He enjoyed a career of success in Rome following the death of Nero and his own emancipation and there cultivated his own addendums to the original tenets of Stoicism.

UNFORTUNATELY, the political tides of Rome changed with every new emperor, and following the collapse of the Julio-Claudian dynasty, a series of weak and ineffective rulers succeeded each other. The Year of the Four emperors saw rapid and predictable shifts in the political climate of the empire, with each bringing his own ideologies and ways of thought to the imperial offices of Rome. Following that horrid year, in which Galba seized power from Nero, and was in turn murdered by Otho, who fell victim to Vitellius, who was killed by the troops loyal to Vespasian, the Flavians established a somewhat stable series of rulers to run the empire, and life began to return to normal.

DURING THIS TIME, Epictetus taught in Rome, preached his own version of Stoicism. It is known that he studied for a time under Musonius Rufus, a mostly forgotten senator who won little favor or popularity among his peers due to his way of thinking. Despite his newfound freedom, Epictetus did not find life in Rome as a freedman all that pleasant.

THE JULIO-CLAUDIAN RULERS—ENLIGHTENED, if not always humane, and given over to the pursuit of arts and culture—were favorable to philosophy and fostered its growth and propagation within the fledgling empire. But the Flavian were rulers of a different sort. Militaristic and sculpted by the violent times from which they rose, emperors such as Vespasian and Domitian dominated Roman political life for nearly thirty years and, in that span of time, issued such decrees as Domitian's edict banning philosophers not only from Rome but from the entire Italian peninsula in 89 AD.

. . .

FOLLOWING this ban of wisdom from the streets of Rome, Epictetus and many other philosophers were lucky to escape Domitian's reign with their lives and fled to all corners of the known world. Epictetus himself landed in northwest Greece, where he lived and taught and eventually died sometime in the first half of the second century AD. He left behind a large base of scholars to spread his views on Stoicism and the nature of man, which were recorded and exist in fragmentary documents to this day.

EPICTETUS SAW many facets of human nature, from his dark days as the chattel property of a Roman lord in service to a deranged emperor, to his prominence as a philosopher in the post-Nero days, and then again in his exile to Greece, where the only surviving records of his teachings were written down by a young pupil named Arrian. The strange and ever-changing times in which he lived, and his own personal experience, naturally affected his world view and gave rise to new conceptions of Zeno's Stoic philosophy. Many scholars today see him as the heir apparent to the throne of Stoicism, carrying on the work of Zeno's generation through his adherence to Stoic thought.

. . .

LIKE MANY PHILOSOPHERS of his time, Epictetus established in his work a dichotomy between what was good and what wasn't. This constant conflict between that which was or wasn't good created the ills of the world in that the choices available to men and women lead to mistakes and errors in judgment. Errors in judgment lead humanity to covet that which was good for neither individual men, nor mankind as a whole. In his attempt to rectify these errors in judgment made by humankind throughout the ages, he wrote lengthy discourses about what exactly was *good*. What defined it? Where did it come from and who got to determine whether one thing was good or not?

THESE QUESTIONS PUZZLED many Hellenistic philosophers, from Aristotle and Socrates through Epictetus himself and beyond. The answer to this question of what can be considered good is in large part the root of the Stoic movement and their disavowal of the pursuit of wealth and property.

. . .

THE STOICS—EPICTETUS among them—declared that
only righteous and virtuous action could be considered wholly good because they alone benefited all
who held them, all who lived by the strictures of
virtue and moral responsibility. Wealth could not be
defined as such because wealth, for many individuals, provides the basis of moral corruption and can
even be the seed of one's own destruction. This idea
is reflected in Zeno's conversion to a life of asceticism following his shipwreck: all the gold he made
trading couldn't save him from the powers of Posei-
don. Likewise, as a former slave, Epictetus was fully
aware of how the concepts of ownership, possession,
and dominion ran against the grain of how man
should act according to the laws of reason as laid out
by generations of philosophers who came before.

HIS STATUS as a former freed slave also had obvious
implications on other facets of his thought. He wrote
heavily about another concept that has been
inherent to Stoicism through all of its incarnations
over the years: the admission that some things
simply lie beyond the control of the individuals
affected by them.

. . .

THE STOICS BELIEVED that another of humanity's great faults lied in the fact that man, through history, has sought to change circumstances that one simply cannot exert any control over. This theme is echoed through countless pieces of Greek drama, *Oedipus Rex*, serving as a noteworthy example. Building off this theme, Epictetus held that humans, for all our brainpower and elevated thought, actually have control over very little. This may sound dour to the modern thinker in the twenty-first century, but at the turn of millennium and shortly after, this thought afforded philosophers such as Epictetus the notion that, if we only have power over that which resides in our own minds, and nothing else, then the only just endeavor to spend one's life on was the pursuit of knowledge and the temperance of the passions that ravaged one's logical mind.

THE TROUBLES of the outside should offer no trouble to the Stoic sage because they are not within the sage's own control. Only the sage's *reaction* to those circumstances are controllable and, therefore, only those reactions are worthy of the sage's attention and cultivation.

. . .

THE CONTRIBUTIONS of Epictetus to Stoic thought, quite literally, fills volumes, and cannot be covered entirely here, but overall, he has left an impression of the philosophy of the Stoic movement that is valid today. His attempts at living an honest Stoic life and the effects of those radical lifestyle changes made him at the same an iconoclastic hero of the academia of imperial Rome, and anathema to those who sought to preserve social norms and customs. Though little is known about his life and times, we know today that his extremely influential thought helped to steer the course of subsequent Stoic philosophers.

SENECA THE YOUNGER

Living in the days of Julius and Augustus Caesar, Seneca the Younger inherited as a philosopher a social and political climate that fostered deep thought and introspection among the Roman elite. As a scholar, he grew up under the tutelage of the upper-class Roman imperials, for whom the pursuit of philosophy was considered a bona fide path to power and respect among society.

. . .

AT THE TIME, the Romans broke with older customs and began writing philosophy in Latin, rather than the original Greek, and the wave of intellectualism that spread with the rising of the newfound empire fueled not only his philosophical learnings but also a robust and virile political career that saw him serving the administration of Nero before his exile for the crime of adultery with a woman of the imperial family (Vogt, 2016).

IN HIS LIFE, he lived through five emperors and numerous political upheavals, such as the temperance of Augustus and his Pax Romana, the mad reign of Caligula, and the Pisonian conspiracy to murder Nero, for which he was convicted and compelled to commit suicide in 65 AD (Vogt, 2016). Though his political success was limited by his exile in 41 AD, he continued for another two decades to learn and teach in the old empire, engendering developments in Stoic philosophy that would late influence scholars such as Epictetus and Musonius Rufus. This life of ups and down, intense passion and violence informed his writing. Through the production of a series of well-known ancient dramas, as well as an extensive collection of letters that still exist today, Seneca the Younger carried Zeno's Stoic torch to the new millennium, adjusting the philosophy for a new era, and making groundbreaking strides toward creating a philosophy that could be adopted by the masses.

HIS WORK DID MUCH to shed light on the new Roman intellectualism, which was considered by many to be a school of upstarts that paled in comparison to the "real" philosophers of Greece, who wrote in the old language and studied in the old schools.

BUT THE CHANGES in lifestyle experienced by the upper echelon of early imperial Rome did away with the notion that learning needed to take place in a school. Seneca the Younger capitalized of the patronage of rich Romans—himself born into wealth and title—and helped construct a new philosophical paradigm that allowed for philosophy to be enacted in policy, in warfare, in daily life.

. . .

Essentially, his philosophy consisted of philosophy in action. He preached practicality and often disavowed the overblown intellectual phantasms that made ancient philosophy obtuse to the public. He intertwined various aspects of Stoic thought with other fields of philosophical inquiry and is known as an independent thinker in that he took influence from early Stoics while not hesitating to disagree with certain maxims that he felt had ceased to function as effective or therapeutic ideologies in his own contemporary era.

As a result, his writing is not bogged down by the epistemological and ontological origins of free will, nor does he stumble over clunky definitions that obfuscate the meaning of his message. Rather, he writes clearly, in Latin, about how one can employ philosophy toward a better world and healthier moral life. His accessible writing style invites readers to participate in the philosophy itself and holds that mere acceptance of values and virtues as delineated by scholars who came before does not inherently equate to an honest appropriation of philosophical thought into one's life (Vogt, 2016).

. . .

SENECA'S HUMANISTIC WRITING, often centered around an imagined debater's own difficulties in life, does not just spout maxims and ideals with no context, but rather, puts his readers in the mind of a person suffering from the existential crises that mattered most to Ancient Romans and, therefore, serves the public as an example of how one actually goes about living a virtuous life.

HIS MOST NOTEWORTHY contributions to Stoic thought lie in his discourses on the nature of the human soul, its purpose as a vehicle for free will, and the psychological aspects of the human condition. He writes that it is not enough to follow an argument or debate principles, but that the conclusions one comes to must be enacted in order for the soul— which he perceives to be one wholly rational body housed within the human corpus—to fully experience the benefits of a good life. It is not the debate itself, but the *effects* of the debate in the debater's later actions that determine whether philosophical inquiry leads to a better life. This notion of the soul as one, often referred to as psychological monism, and its dependency of philosophically informed action is in step with traditional Stoic thought in that it induces readers to adopt these ideas as a way of life.

SENECA ALSO MADE major contributions to philosophy's perception of human emotions, and his work in this field of Stoicism has contributed largely to its evolution through the ages.

THE FIRST WAVE of Stoic philosophers posited that human emotion held the seat of irrational thought and action, and the pursuit of life lived in accordance with such emotions served to damage the virtues of man. In order to live a life of temperance, emotional responses had to be moderated and kept in check, had to be held back and augmented so as to prevent those emotions from clouding the rational outlook of one's soul. But Seneca argued that it was impossible to moderate emotions. They existed within the realm of the irrational, and therefore, could not be moderated. According to Seneca, "the ideal agent will avenge and defend others out of a sense of duty, not out of anger or lust for revenge" (Vogt, 2016).

· · ·

Through his tragedies and his epistles, Seneca makes great strides in humanity's understanding of emotions and the power of agency they have over human thought. He wrote clearly and with lucidity so his message would be received by a vast number of people and, in doing so, helped contribute to the survival of the Stoic way of life and thought during the political turbulence of ancient Imperial Rome. Centuries later, his work would still be studied and continued to be influential, and his thoughts certainly provided a large base of work on which later Stoics such as Epictetus would build.

Marcus Aurelius

Though many philosophers might have done more scholarship than Marcus Aurelius, none theorized from such lofty heights as the final emperor to partake in Augustus Caesar's Pax Romana. Ascending to the throne in 161 AD and ruling for almost two decades, Marcus Aurelius is remembered by historians in a most contradictory light: some view his contributions to the art of leadership and temperance as the height of enlightened wisdom, and in this regard view Marcus Aurelius as history's most pure manifestation of Aristotle's philosopher king. This does not cloud the judgment of all historians, however. His attitude towards Christians stands in stark contrast with his beneficent views of women, orphans, and slaves, and his disavowal of the classic Stoic mindset of philosophy as a way of life rather than as a system of thought is believed by some to be the seed of the Roman Empire's decline following the Pax Romana (Noyen, 1955).

AS AN EMPEROR, he contributed to the persecution of Christians within the empire, widespread reform to the Roman legal system in a pre-Justinian era, and fought off both internal Italian revolts as well as German invasions into the hinterlands of the empire. His reign was considered to be rather peaceful, and he is remembered by history, for the most part, fondly.

AS A PHILOSOPHER, Marcus Aurelius expounded the ideals of the old Stoic philosophers from previous centuries. He is a noted disciple of both Seneca and Epictetus, and his works feature heavily quoted passages from the original Stoics in Greece (Komtekar, 2018). In his *Meditations*, he writes of the classic Stoic ideals, namely, that "the world is governed by Providence, that happiness lies in virtue, which is wholly in one's own power, and that one should be angry with one's associates" (Komtekar, 2018).

HIS THOUGHTS in *Meditations* raise very serious moral questions about the validity of Stoic thought and call into question the notion of pleasure's inherent goodness and pain's inherent evil. Such a black and white dichotomy, argues Marcus, can lead to impious questioning of the order of nature, which, at root, is the basis of the entire philosophy. What is a Stoic to do about the benefits bestowed upon an evil man while a good man suffers? This question gets at the heart of Stoicism's grave flaw. Should a philosopher ignore this injustice? To do otherwise would be to give in to passion which engenders the paradox that drove Marcus Aurelius to direct his philosophical, rambling and sometimes incoherent texts toward the rule of law and the governance of a just society.

.   .   .

AS A LEADER OF THE PEOPLE, he enacted hundreds of new laws within the empire to benefit the lesser classes of Romans, and this contributes greatly to his remembrance as a benevolent, tempered philosopher king in the vein of Aristotelian notions of rulership.

EXPANDING UPON THIS IDEA, he writes about the roles of individuals and their respective responsibility toward the community within which they live. According to Kamtekar, Marcus Aurelius disavowed the notion of an individual existing separate from the greater society that gave rise to that individual's thoughts, experiences, emotional reactions, and worldviews. This runs contrary to traditional Stoic thought in that it places people within the context of the society from which they view the world. In this regard, the lack of agency in determining outward change in the world, a primary tenet of Stoicism, is reduced, and agency is granted to mankind in its ability to alter human society.

ACCORDING TO AURELIUS, we are, in a sense, inescapably products of our environment, and as such, we owe a debt to our society to act on its behalf. In keeping with original Stoic thought, he did not view this maxim as merely applying to Romans within the boundaries of the empire, but as applying to individuals as citizens of a greater world society.

HE STRONGLY ENDORSED the Greek notion of the *cosmopolitan*, which held that people are not citizens of one city or another, this province or that, but rather exist as citizens of the world. Though he is often criticized for failing to live up to the Stoic ethos of living out philosophy through daily action, his ideology regarding the cosmopolitan requires that man helps his fellow man, and posits that we all share the same struggles, are indebted to one another for support, and that humans are honor-bound to bring about those indifferents which are favorable to their entire society.

THIS EGALITARIAN APPROACH to the role of man in a rational universe can be observed in his legal code, which promised sweeping rights to the disenfranchised and sought to make Roman life more conducive to community involvement and betterment. In this regard, we can hear his philosophy echoing through the ages in the voice of Immanuel Kant, whose categorical imperative urges people to only act in a way that would be appropriate for the benefit of everyone.

THOUGH HE HAS OFTEN BEEN CRITICIZED by modern historians for expounding at great length about philosophical virtues while not exactly living up to the teachings, his reign is noted for the philanthropy and goodwill he extended toward the lesser classes of Roman society. Women, orphans, and slaves are the subjects of a vast majority of his legal writings, and his reign saw many benefits for them encoded in the legal apparatus of the empire (Kamtekar, 2018).

HE ENACTED legal codes that made slaves not only an object about law revolved, but a subject in which they were active players. He granted rights of freedom to slaves who were promised such by masters, and he passed legislation that helped Roman society break away from the old patriarchal ways and forge a new path in which mothers and women, in general, were more respected agents in household affairs.

THE PHILOSOPHY OF THE STOA

When Zeno of Citium first began preaching his Stoic philosophy, the social conditions of Ancient Greece were not unlike the conditions that exist within the western world of the twenty-first century. Corruption in both the government and the upper echelons of society ran rampant, and men held the esteem of temples and politicians in higher regard than they did the good of the world as a whole. In the introduction of his fiery and iconoclastic discourse, *The Republic*, he rails against these societal woes and promises to envisage a society free from such ill-fated trappings. His writing in regard to the societal structure and the institutions at work in ancient Greek society were seen as inflammatory, and many found his views to be overly idealistic and not based in reality.

DESPITE THE PERCEIVED flaws that were delineated by his detractors, this work is known as the seminal philosophical text on Stoicism from the Hellenistic period and is seen by both contemporaneous Greek philosophers and modern-day historians as an attack on Plato's influential work of the same name. In the Platonic Republic, the wise rule all, and the systems of society are established within the framework of oligarchy, whereas Zeno imagined the perfect society to be a world in which there was only the wise, and they ruled themselves without the aid of governmental organizations or bodies (Erskine, 2000).

INTERESTINGLY ENOUGH, the manner in which they organize their imaginary societies is reflective of the manner in which they went about their philosophies. In Zeno's republic, the power is shared by all, just as his brand of philosophy was spread through the streets for all to hear and listen. There is no need for rulers because everyone has been inculcated with the steadfast belief in the supremacy of the rational. This is juxtaposed by the Platonic oligarchy, which is representative of the closed-door teaching methods prominent in his school. Societal institutions seen as intrinsic to man's nature, such as marriage and currency, have no value in Zeno's republic because they, to the Stoic philosopher, provide man with nothing but an escape from the virtuous life into a life of hedonistic passion.

AT THE TIME, Zeno's new philosophy—his inflammatory answer to the current mode of thinking prevalent in Ancient Greece at the time—created scandal and controversy, and angered many philosophers who found the ideas contained therein to be juvenile and lacking in depth. But in order to understand why this philosophy created such a stir in Greek culture, we will have to inspect its tenets and values and determine why such views would be both lambasted and ridiculed while simultaneously gaining enough followers to steer the course of philosophical inquiry for centuries to come.

. . .

PRIMARILY, the Stoic philosophers beginning with Zeno of Citium divided philosophy into the study of reason or logic, the study of physics and the natural order of the world through which mankind operates, and the study of ethical action and the nature of wrongdoing, or evil.

HE HELD that the ultimate pursuit of the sage's life was to live virtuously, and this could only be attained by living in accordance with reason, which is the man's place in the natural order of the world. In this way, we can begin to see the basics of the philosophy being fleshed out. We start with a universe and rational order that enacts itself upon that universe. From this supposition, we come to the role of man within that universal framework. This role is a direct extension of the universe itself.

FINALLY, we come to the aim of man's role, to attain virtue through a philosophically introspective life. With this sort of order imposed on the world around him, Zeno built the basics of a philosophy that sought to place the natural world as a prime directive, as an original mover. It is from the ordering of the universe that everything else springs forth. Perhaps this notion speaks to why we have no agency in controlling the world. In the end, everything going on around us has a performative role in our lives as the schematic by which we subconsciously live.

THOUGH MANY PEOPLE have amended Zeno's original philosophy over the years, and his own work did not survive through the tides of history, we can infer many things about his teaching through the disciples that he left in his wake. Put simply, in the original incarnation of Zeno's Stoicism, students are presented with the notion of man as being apart from the lower order animals of the world in that man has the ability to practice reason. This is the basis of a great distinction between Zeno and the beliefs of other philosophers at the time.

EPICUREAN THOUGHT HELD THAT MANKIND, in order to achieve happiness, must analyze its own inherent wants, the objects that drive its desires, and order life around the pursuit of those objects of desire. For Zeno, however, this worldview ignored the primary difference between man and beast: that man had logic and reason, and that man's order in the natural world was inseparable from that ability of rational thought. Though the Stoics and the Epicureans held many similar beliefs in regard to the nature of the universe, they applied these structures to the human condition in dramatically different ways.

To the hedonistic Epicureans, if an infant child is driven toward natural pleasure such as food, water, and the safety of a mother's touch, all of these things must be for the betterment of man. Since those are mankind's basest desires, and the first thing that even a child implicitly knows without being taught, the pursuit of pleasure should stand as an example for humankind in maturity. Epicurus believed that by depriving humans of that from which they derive pleasure, society engenders the problems of the world.

In contrast, Zeno held that those selfsame pursuits are what engendered the worst aspects of human cruelty, greed, and licentiousness. The unbridled pursuit of passions, in the Stoic mindset, refuted the primacy of human logic and effaced the divinity of providence that man obviously possessed. It is because of this that Zeno embraced asceticism so fully in his philosophy. The only thing that humanity could truly do to better its condition was to live in reason and cultivate a view conducive to the practicing of rational discourse. Everything else was merely a distraction from the true Stoic goal of achieving a virtuous life.

IN REGARD to the laws of nature and the physics of the universe, as the Stoics understood them, it was mankind's providential place in the cosmos to pursue its reason with the full force of its developmental psychological understanding. It was self-preservation to live a rational, mediated life because it was that life that we naturally inherited from our god given abilities to reason. For the Stoics, the philosophical life, the pursuit of the sages, revolves around reason, virtue, and the natural order of the world around them. The divinity of the cosmos and the immanence of the gods factored heavily into their beliefs, and in the later years of antiquity, Stoicism began to undertake the task of psychological reckoning, trying to determine the seat of happiness and the conflict of emotion and reason.

IN THIS CHAPTER, we'll get at the heart of what it meant to Zeno to be a Stoic, and how that ideal was shaped by the Classical and Hellenistic teachings that preceded Zeno.

THE ETHICS of Virtue

Ethics in the Stoic worldview, just like the Epicurean worldview, revolved around what it meant to feel happy. What caused happiness and what were its purposes and functions in a rational, human world? To speak of this quality of content-ment, the Stoics used *eudaimonia* to describe the sense of happiness that arose from a virtuous life lived with a keen eye to the Stoic ethical framework (Baltzly, 2019).

IN ORDER TO ACHIEVE *EUDAIMONIA*, one must secure the possession of that which benefits the possessor in every circumstance. According to the disciples of

Zeno, that which benefits the possessor at every turn can only be one thing: virtue.

FOR THE STOICS, virtue was the building block upon which philosophy was erected. For the Epicureans, who dominated intellectual thought in the days prior to Zeno, material wealth, sex, good food, wine, and power—all these things led to happiness because to possess them was enjoyable. Everyone loved to eat good food, to attend a party, to enjoy relations with one's wife. These things were good and they were healthy, and they were the end product of a life well-lived.

ZENO UPTURNED the philosophical world of his day by contending that these things weren't *good*, but rather fell into the category of that which was actually *indifferent*. Possessing wealth and a beautiful wife did not secure happiness for everyone at every turn and, therefore, according to the philosophy of the Stoa, were not basely good. They may have aided in the achieving of happiness for a select few fortunate enough to possess them, but plenty of instances of wealth causing corruption and anguish, in the end, provided Zeno with the backbone upon which he built his ascetic philosophy and helped him reach the conclusion that the only thing in the world, in the entire human universe, that was truly and wholly *good* was the pursuit of virtue.

VIRTUE in a Stoic framework can be seen as an umbrella term that covers those functions of the human mind that separate man and animal. Courage, excellence of thought, purity, moderation of impulse: all of these things fell into the category of virtuous attributes under Zeno's school of thought. This is because they were derived from man's ability to reason and think rationally.

IN STUDYING THE STOIC WORLDVIEW, we are again confronted by a major difference in the teachings of both Zeno and Epicurus. Zeno pointed out that beings with souls—animals and humans—did not pursue that which was pleasurable for them when in a state of nature, but that which aided in their survival. Surely, a lion fighting and dying to defend its cubs does not view the experience as pleasurable but will engage in such behavior anyway, out of a sense of preservation not only for itself but for its kin as well. Likewise, individual humans can pursue wealth and power, but these in themselves do not serve the survival of either himself or his community.

THUS, for the Stoics, happiness did not derive itself from pleasure, but rather from a life of reason, and a life of reasonable inquiry demanded respect for those qualities which one might deem virtuous. From this idea, the Stoics came to the conclusion that asceticism was the true path of the sage, and to forego behaviors that contributed to the corrupt and morally bankrupt state of affairs in Greece at that time was the only behavior of a being bent on adhering to the law of rationality.

THE STRENGTH of Fortitude Against Negative Emotions

Taking the Stoic love of rationality and virtue into practice in the real world can seem difficult in the midst of consumer culture, and certainly the original Stoics of the second and third centuries BCE had a hard time getting others on board with a philosophy that seemed so dour and unenjoyable in the face of Epicurean hedonism. But the joys of Stoicism and its practical use as a determinant of human thought and action cut deeper than pleasure alone, and through its implementation, stoic thought leads to happiness in a more roundabout, obtuse way.

BY PRACTICING the values of Stoicism and attempting to lead a virtuous life as laid out by Zeno and his followers, we are confronted with the problem of evil in the world. Negative emotions of pain and anger and lust are innate to the human condition and it takes a true sage to do away with their influence, but the Stoics preached that by adhering to reason, a sage can free himself from all negative emotions and take the world at "face value" so to speak. By accepting the presence of evil and negativity in the world, the Stoics freed themselves from its bonds and allowed for a greater psychological and metaphysical discourse to arise from its presence.

. . .

TAKE EPICTETUS, for example. Born a slave and made to endure the greatest of hardships, to overcome the loftiest obstacles to man's happiness, Epictetus had every reason to wallow in hedonism after being freed, though he chose instead to continue his life of Stoic reasoning in keeping with the teachings of Zeno because, like all good Stoics, Epictetus believed that negative emotions result from the misconception that happiness is something to be *gained* through interaction with the outside world rather than something to be discovered through meditation and the art of self-cultivation.

TO THE STOIC, adversity such as slavery or war or famine are functions of the world that we have no control over. We are acted upon by these forces and have no recourse to them, but we are able to control our reactions. By maintaining a sense of fortitude, Stoics ensure that they are unaffected by the trials of daily life.

THE EFFICACY of Stoicism as a means of handling adversity is evinced by the life stories of so many prominent Stoics. The brutality of the ancient world gave rise to many occasions for meditation on the nature of evil and how to handle its presence in one's life. Through their collective experiences, the Stoics naturally evolved a sense of fortitude housed within their philosophical doctrines that aimed at making man's mental state impervious to outward strife. This is in keeping with Eastern philosophy and is one of the primary connections between the Hellenistic schools of thought discussed in this book and other philosophies such as Taoism or Buddhism.

THIS BELIEF EMBODIES a main tenet of Stoicism as a philosophy in practice. It relies on the Stoic supposition that emotions are not enacted on humans or the product of outside forces exerting energy on the human soul, but are rather the product of the human soul itself, and fall within the realm of that which can be controlled by human temperance. By adjusting the manner in which one reacts to grievances, inconveniences, tragedies and the like, one can temper their emotions and bring about a more rational discourse surrounding the origins of the discontent.

. . .

50

THE STOIC CALL for a regulation of the emotions has often been bastardized over the centuries and is in large part one of the reasons for the backlash against Stoic thought during the period of European history spanning the Renaissance and the Enlightenment. Thinkers of those times simply did not believe that negating passion would lead to a better way of life. But this is a misconception, for Stoics don't preach the disavowal and negation of emotions completely. As already noted, Seneca believed that any attempt to moderate one's emotions was doomed to fail because they, by nature, existed outside the realm of reason and could not, therefore, be controlled by reasonable thought alone.

RATHER THAN DOING AWAY with emotion completely, the Stoic philosophy holds that by tempering our reactions and perceptions, by ignoring preconceived notions and societal norms related to things such as the commission of a crime or the existence of corruption, we can change the manner in which these evils affect us. We can learn to adopt a position of Stoic apathy toward both positive and negative passions, and thereby learn the sage-like wisdom preached by Zeno. This notion appears frequently throughout the ages, from Epictetus through Seneca, and is a cornerstone of the philosophy.

IN A SENSE, fortitude against negative emotions is the endgame of Stoic philosophy. In a world beset by the evils of corrupted human emotions and the derivative actions precipitated by such emotions, Stoicism offers a way out for those who seek to better themselves and, by extension, the world around them. This is why Seneca argues that the sage does not react adversely to the ills of the human condition such as vice, war, and grief of mourning, but rather, "puts on a smile…because his cheerfulness gives hope" (Vogt, 2016).

HIS THOUGHTS in this regard are a perfect example of how Stoicism exists in the world not only as a philosophy to be debated over by intellectuals but also as a guide to teach the layman about leading a virtuous life with an aim to benefit himself and others around him. An adverse situation may arise, but by adjusting one's perception of that adversity, one frees oneself from the preconceived notion that negative input must result in a negative output.

. . .

A WRONG IS NOT MADE right by an additional wrong, in the Stoic worldview, and the only way to rationally confront adversity is to remember that by not letting one's emotional reaction to the stimulus run wild, one can bear even the hardship of Epictetus in fetters, or Seneca in the mad court of a murderous emperor.

NATURALISM and the Stoic Worldview

There is no way to discuss the naturalism of the Stoics without discussing their belief in gods. To the Stoics, the universe is of a divine nature, mediated and governed by the principles of a deity or deities and serving the purpose laid out by that deity. Humans fit into this world as rational creatures gifted our rationality by a benevolent god. In this way, philosophers such as Epictetus view human thought as a sort of an offshoot of the same divine providence that is at work in the ordering of the universe. God for the Stoics represents the life and vitality of the universe and exists both corporeally and as a divine substance within us.

. . .

ONE OF THE curiosities of the Stoic physics lies in the biological orientation on their views regarding the nature of deities. For the Stoics, God (or gods) were material beings, comprised of the same atoms that made up the world, man, and the cosmos. Furthermore, the nature of deities is likened to a fire, bringing life and warmth to that which it endeavors to create.

BECAUSE THE DEITIES of the Stoics were wholly rational beings, and the rational arrangement of the universe springs forth from the rational nature of the deity responsible for its creation, ancient followers of Zeno described God as a sort of "hot breath" or fiery *pneuma*. This definition may, in large part, be inspired by early Hellenistic medicinal theory, and their reliance on such a biologically oriented cosmos establishes a major doctrinal dissonance between other philosophies at the time.

THE EPICUREANS BELIEVED that god was material, similar to the beliefs of the Stoics, but for them, the deities were not rational beings who instilled their rationality in their own creations. Rather,

Epicureans believed that the ordering of the cosmos was random, the function of atomic collision as ancient Greeks understood it, and the creator deity was an uncaring being that had long since detached itself from the fates and tempers of humanity.

IN CHRISTIANITY, God is a benevolent, conscious deity not dissimilar from the Stoic incarnation, but the similarities end there. The Christian god is wholly apart from individual man. This makes a big difference in the manner in which these two schools of thought interact with the question of providence. The Stoics assert that, in a sense, we all have a piece of god within us. We all contain that seed of rationality with which we were endowed through a rational god. Christians, on the other, hold God to be an unachievable state of perfection that cannot be aspired to by man.

PERHAPS THE STOIC view regarding deities and their nature contributed to the longstanding survival of the philosophy as a way of life. By taking the powers of a deity and instilling it in the very soul of humankind, Stoics create a worldview that enables its adherents to participate in the divine order of things, rather than watch as a passive observer.

THE INACCESSIBILITY of the Christian god and the uncaring nature of the Epicurean god makes the Stoic interpretation of such themes more inviting and more conducive to self-improvement. By placing the qualities of god squarely within the human soul, Stoic philosophy engenders a greater sense of agency in determining one's fate. The same "thought processes," for lack of a better term, that were at work in the creation of the universe are also at work within the creation of thought, emotion, and human personality.

THIS HAS AN EMPOWERING effect on the believer in that it makes room for the universal "oneness" that is crucial to the Stoic frame of mind in regard to the organization of the universe. Because the rational deity responsible for creating the universe endowed his own characteristics within his creation, everything in the universe exists with a sort of harmony that informs Stoic notions such as the primacy of rationality.

. . .

SENECA ALSO WROTE HEAVILY about the natural law as viewed by Stoic philosophy, both in respect as a source of fear for humans and its position in relation to the deterministic worldview preached by the philosophy.

FOR SENECA, the "fetus already contains the seed of its death, the beginnings of the world contain its end" (Vogt 2016). To put this position in line with the rest of the philosophy, it can be asserted that if the world is a deterministic place by its very nature as the product of rational, reasonable ordering as ordained by Zeus, then the forces of nature and the effects of those forces on the human world can be viewed by the Stoic in much the same way the Stoic views the acquisition of money or property: it is neither good nor evil, but indifferent.

IT FALLS into the field of things that cannot be controlled, and therefore, should serve the Stoic by reminding him that aspects of death and natural disasters are preordained by the deities and are final judgments that humankind has no power over. Put into action within their moral framework, this notion allows the Stoic to view death, not as a tragedy, but rather as a sort of rite or ritual that everyone partakes in, everyone is a part of.

IN SENECA, the purpose of the natural world is to remind humanity of its own mortality. The seasons of the year, the dangers of high tide, the seemingly random events of the Ancient Greek world such as earthquakes or volcanic eruptions are just incarnations of the divine providence that set the world in motion in the first place. This idea is used to further bolster the arguments of equality made by many Stoic thinkers. If death is the great equalizer, and a shared experience of rich and poor, freemen and slaves, then to what degree do the societal positions occupied by a person during his or her lifetime actually determine that person's quality of life?

THIS IDEAL IS ECHOED in Marcus Aurelius' *Meditations* when he poses the question of "providence or atoms" as the determining factor of the order of the universe. Whether or not the universe and its contents follow the Stoic way of thought—being designed by providence—or the Epicurean idea that they are the product of atomic collisions in an otherwise random void of space, Marcus Aurelius uses the Stoic worldview to argue that the trappings of contemporary society in second century Rome must be indifferent because there is no reasonable allocation of these resources among good and evil men.

THIS IS an example of Marcus Aurelius grappling with his Stoic teachings in his journal and attempting to come to a philosophical resolution about the nature of good and evil, using the naturalistic frame of mind first posited by Zeno. He argues for a providential world and states that the pursuit of happiness through hedonistic excess must be a gateway to false happiness simply because such pursuits are not in line with the Stoic belief about the physics of the world. If wealth is not evenly distributed in accordance with man's rationality and virtue, he states, it must not "good" in the original stoical sense of the word to pursue such things. These pursuits would run contrary to the natural order, and they are an efface to the divinity of the providential arrangement of the cosmos and the world.

THAT GOD IS central to both the natural and human world is a staple tenet of the Stoic ecological world-view, but it does not encapsulate all of their thoughts regarding the functional nature of our world. Stoics also believed in the cyclical nature of the planet as evinced by the human lifecycle and other empirical observations of the world around them, and these beliefs carried implications for their ethical and philosophical diatribes.

THIS RECOGNITION of the world's cyclical structure later informed their thoughts on causation and determinism and was a grounding piece of informa-tion taken as an accepted premise when they discussed or debated God's role in the determining of the events of the universe.

FOR THE STOIC, despite the fact that the world in which we live is so heavily determined by the events, people, and things that have come before us and helped to shape the milieu we inherit, the actions a person chooses to takes are just as much the product of their own decision making, their own experience, and their own virtues as they are a function of fate or determinism.

THIS IS BECAUSE, to a Stoic, one's reactions, will, and thoughts are entirely up to oneself, and the deterministic nature of the universe does not equate to a world in which people have no agency over their actions or thoughts.

MODERN STOICISM

*A*s mentioned earlier, Stoicism as a philosophy, an educational framework, and a way of life featured heavily in the Ancient World, from Greece to Rome. Its influences are widespread, and the accessibility of ancient teachers to held seminars and discussions in public spaces offered the public a view of philosophy in action that earlier thinkers such as Aristotle and Plato could not offer the populace because of their closed-door privacy and organization of educational institutions in Ancient Greece.

BECAUSE ZENO WAS an iconoclast who sought to upend the intellectual world with his way of life and his teachings, he became a public figure to the people of Athens and his teachings were remembered and adhered to by a large number of people.

MOVING BEYOND ANTIQUITY, Stoicism seems to have fallen out of vogue and was largely ignored or forgotten throughout the centuries of Christian hegemony during the Middle Ages. Questions of God's corporeality and the physical nature of the soul were troubling to Middle Age philosophers and these views were often seen as contradictory to the church's teachings, flagrant and offensive to those who studied the art of knowledge in monasteries, under the watchful eyes of abbots who controlled the means of publication and dissemination of information in an age with nonexistent printing technology.

THESE CONTRADICTIONS between the ancient way of thinking and the more modern Judo-Christian worldview gave rise to a school of thought in the sixteenth and seventeenth centuries known as Neostoicism.

. . .

THE NEOSTOICS WERE a group of philosophers who sought to merge the two discourses into one unified field of study that would embody the teachings of both disciplines while providing adherents with a means to make sense of the drastic and brutal religious violence that swept Europe during the 1500s and early 1600s. The founding father of Neostoicism, Justus Lipsius, was a born Catholic in modern-day Belgium, though he amended his faith and changed allegiances many times during his life. Because of this, many contemporaries criticized his philosophy and sought to downplay the importance of his work.

DESPITE CONTEMPORANEOUS DISAVOWAL of his religious principles, Justus Lipsius still became a philosopher of note and has left a lasting impression of study of Stoicism through his work analyzing Seneca.

IN MANY WAYS, the times in which he lived affected the course of his philosophical leanings, and today he is remembered as an antidote to the brutality of philosophers like Machiavelli (Papy, 2019). A life-long advocate of monarchism based on Stoic principles, he released political writings aimed at subverting the idea promulgated in Machiavelli's seminal book, *The Prince*.

ABSOLUTE MONARCHY SHOULD NOT BE BASED on the acquisition of power, according to Lipsius, but rather on the tempered and Stoic emotional responses of a truly just ruler.

GIVEN the times in which he lived, it is not hard to imagine why Justus Lipsius wanted to write about the origins of political power and the balance of power between absolute monarchs and the subjects they ruled over. With civil war rampant across the European mainland, philosophical exaltations of regicide and revolt were commonplace and many writers argued—in proto-American fashion—that the ability of the people to overthrow an unjust ruler was the only way to prevent rulers from becoming unjust in the first place. To Lipsius, this was an affront to the teachings of Seneca. He proposed that by educating the royalty of Europe in such teachings, the need for rebellion would be moot and that the harmony first envisaged almost two thousand years previously in Zeno's *Republic* would be a plausible reality.

DESPITE THE FACT that Lipsius never succeeded in bringing about the rise of the Stoic monarchy, his teachings remained influential for centuries after his death, and prominent moral philosophers of later periods are indebted to his work for their own conceptions of justice, virtue, and human nature.

HIS WRITING LAID the groundwork for the humanist movement and the Enlightenment, and in many ways, propagated the original Stoic teachings, even if he attempted to merge them to Christian ethics with which they were blatantly incompatible.

IN MORE RECENT DECADES, Stoicism has experienced another renaissance and is once again an active school of thought with practitioners seeking to enhance their own lives and the lives of those around them. It has evolved from Zeno's original incarnation to be more applicable to life in the modern world, but the core tenets remain the same: the world acts according to its own nature, and as participants in this world, we are subjected to that nature, for good or ill. It is not the sage's place in the world to fret over what can't be changed, but to modify that which can in the effort of achieving Stoic happiness.

THIS IS EMBODIED through the practical applications of psychotherapy and cognitive behavioral therapy, and, in fact, many of these psychological discourses are influenced by or founded upon some of the principles set forth by the Stoic philosophers of antiquity. Psychological techniques and disciplines that predate cognitive behavioral therapy, such as Albert Ellis' Rational Emotive Therapy (RET) have been in practice since 1955 and are heavily influenced by the work of Stoic philosophers (Ellis, 2007).

FOR THE REMAINDER of this book, we will take what we have learned about the Stoics, their thoughts and lives, and the times in which they lived, and attempt to trace that school of thought's application in the twentieth and twenty-first centuries, and inspect this new amalgam of philosophical and psychological discourse for methods that can be utilized in the interest of leading a more productive, positive life.

You Are Not Always in Control

Albert Ellis, the father of RET and a major early proponent of Stoic thought in modern psychology, argues that humans are driven to action not only by their own knowledge and being, but also by the world around them. The individual responses to given stimuli are the causal descendants not of passive observance of the world, but of the subject's constant desire to create a personal reality around it. Perceptions factor heavily into this framework, and Ellis' notions draw largely from early stoic thought related to the topic of desire. Emotional trouble engendered by failure to achieve goals, lack of success, or the myriad other woes facing us in our modern world today, is rooted in the same problems Epictetus and Zeno encountered in their own cultures.

. . .

BASICALLY, wants and desires do not always conform to reality. Just as the Stoics argued that the world exists outside of humanity and enacts on humanity and that humanity's only rational response to such actions lied in a shifting of perspectives from changing the stimulus to changing the *reaction to the stimulus*, so too does Ellis' RET hold that emotional conditions arise when people refuse to limit their expectation or fail to take the world as it truly is, as an entity outside of one's own control.

So, what are the implications of a world outside of human control? Certainly, in the postmodern era, in the Digital Age, human activity bears so strongly on "the world" that even our climatology and the course of natural disasters seems to be affected. This would seem to detract from what Zeno and Seneca and Marcus Aurelius argue from antiquity, but do their lessons truly hold up in the modern arena? It would seem that, when considering humanity as a whole, so much of the world's ills are firmly within our control, but this would be regarded as an illusion in light of Stoic philosophy.

. . .

THOUGH IT MAY SEEM as if "people" have a great deal of control over the course of history, individual people are often left with little or no agency in a world that is increasingly automated, increasingly bereft of human interaction. To adhere to the original Stoic way of thinking, one would have to first accept that the tide of history act on humans, not the other way around.

THIS IS TRULY NEGATIVE THOUGHT, when approached from through the discourses of modern-day values, and is particularly contentious to the American individualistic worldview that has dominated the past few centuries. But to look at this reflection in a different light would be to rearrange the perspective of the argument: sure, we might not be in control of everything, and much of what we don't have control over does indeed alter or affect the course of our lives, but this reality gives the modern stoic a sense of freedom from the anxiety and stress that is so often associated with the stress of modern life.

WHILE IT IS easy to wallow in despair over faulty automobiles, or the hectic terrors of public transportation, or food shortages and war and the ghost of the Imperial Age still muddying the waters of the Digital Age, it is absolutely difficult to view these stressors as being irreplaceable, innate to the modern human's experience. But if we embrace the stoic teachings of old, we can come to see that not having control over such factors of life gives us the freedom to decide how we want to react.

AND, as so many stoic philosophers have argued in the past, to change how we react is reset the entire paradigm of humanity as an agentless conglomerate. Perhaps by refusing to be ruffled by the trials of life, we can come to a point of recognition where we acknowledge that those selfsame trials causing so much distress are, in fact, just another layer of life, and, as such, are easily disregarded as only tangential to our state of happiness.

SURE, the world is not in your control, but by embracing stoicism, this will cease to matter. The only thing that will matter to the modern Stoic sage is that their reaction to the world *is*. When this reality reaches its fullest potential, it becomes impossible to be bogged down by hazards of life, because what does matter is that we do have control over our emotions, and our emotions, in turn, are responsible for our well-being and happiness.

* * *

Making the Best of the Worst: Conforming to Your Reality

In the modern era, many of Zeno's original doctrines have fallen out of vogue and are no longer considered as vital to the maintenance of happiness or virtue. In the original sense, the way of the sage was fettered by an uncompromising adherence to the laws of nature, which, as defined by early Stoics, entailed living life rationally and in step with their views on ethical discourse.

Considering the scientific advancements and cultural achievements of mankind in the intervening millennia, the worldview and perception of the laws of nature as delineated by the early Stoics can hardly be considered as doctrine. Rather than determining to live in accordance with the laws of universal nature, modern stoicism has decreed that the universe is blatantly and abjectly indifferent to humankind.

THIS OBVIOUSLY RAISES troubling questions for adherence of the old way, as the powerhouses of Stoic philosophy in the Classical and Hellenistic periods all agreed that the rationality of the universe represented a sort of rationality of the human mind, and since both were organized by the same being, both were, in a sense, of a kind. The atrocities committed by man against his fellow man, though not absent from the ancient world, have become stark and clear reminders of the naivete of the old philosophers, and stand as evidence that the world cannot be considered a basely rational or good object.

MODERN STOICISM SEEKS to attach its brand of philosophy to daily life in a manner similar to Zeno of old, but with different aims. Rather than seek to be in harmony with a world that is quite clearly inharmonious, proponents of Modern Stoicism implore adherents to be in harmony with their own particular world.

.   .   .

THE SCHOOL OF MODERN STOICISM, in this way, is an introspective doctrine of self-improvement more than it seeks to be an example of thought that would cure the world's ills. It can almost be said that the echoes of Zeno have grown distorted over the years and that in the modern era, his teachings are aimed at making the world a better place by making its inhabitants a better place, and this can only be done by first being at peace with the social, cultural, emotional, political and psychological world in which individuals reside.

IN ORDER TO be at peace and in a state of acceptance in regard to one's personal environment, an individual must seek to understand that things which cannot be changed must not suffer the attempt. Rather than wasting energy on a fruitless project, the stoic is more content to work on accepting the adversity for what it is, and divesting emotionally passionate responses from one's psychological lexicon when dealing with inalterable adversity.

.   .   .

THIS PHILOSOPHY FREES up energy and creative output that can be dedicated toward more effective and reasonable uses of time and brainpower. If Ellis is right in supposing that unrealistic expectations and ultimatums-in-place-of-goals are the seed of many different types of neuroses, then the act of conforming to one's own personal reality might help to overcome the tribulations associated with major psychological diagnoses (Ellis, 1991).

IN THIS LIGHT, owning one's one reality means coming to terms with one's own skillset, or one's own body type, or one's own background and upbringing, and deciding how to best use those attributes for personal benefits. Only through this path can someone foster agency. If one railed against the attributes of oneself that were inalterable, they would emerge in the psychological landscape as insurmountable hurdles impeding personal and emotional growth. They would become the very stressors that enlightened thinker seeks to challenge.

THE DEVELOPMENT of agency through the acceptance of one's self is an important tenet in the new brand of Stoicism. By developing agency and the ability to act on our own surroundings through both thought and action, we allow ourselves the ability to exercise free will.

Free Will and Emotional Response

Free will is a central tenet to many major philosophies that have captivated the human imagination since the time of the great philosophers of Greece. Christians accepted it as an inheritance from older scholarship, and it served as the main fountain from which evil spouts in the world. 19th-century German philosopher found an agreeable ear in Frederick Nietzsche when he stated that "intellect is not a mirror of the world, but an instrument of the will" (Ure, 2009). Theorizing the intellect of mankind as a tool used by our own free will helps to free the concept of free will from the notion that it is negatively affected by our emotions.

The story of Eve in the Garden of Eden is a common story known throughout the world as a damning assault on the beauty of free will. To Christian theologists, it was Eve's intemperance and her lack of will that led her acceptance the serpent's offer, ruining the innocence of the mankind in the process and establishing the doctrine that free will needs to be reigned in by Christian morality. In this paradigm, free will is either the product or the cause of emotional interference associated with human passion.

FREE WILL IS SEEN by the Stoics in a different light. Going all the way back to Epictetus, mankind's volition has been seen as a positive attribute. It holds us accountable for our actions and gives us the crucial degree of freedom that humans associate with their most natural state.

THE ABILITY TO think for ourselves, define our own realities, and build frameworks of educational, psychological, and philosophical discourse all hinge upon our freedom of choice. For the modern stoic, this is a powerful tool to help mediate a stressful life in today's frenzied atmosphere, The maxim that our will to choose, our ability to deliberate and settle upon that which we find most agreeable, is inherent to our personal identities allows us to reflect not on the role of emotions in determining our will, but rather the role of our will in determining our emotions. It is easy to lose control of one's emotions in the face of seemingly unbearable stress, but by reminding ourselves that we are still accountable for the loss of control and that we have the *power* to choose otherwise, we can mitigate feelings of anger and despair when they arise as the result of negative circumstances.

THOUGH NOT A STOIC HIMSELF, prominent 19th-century philosopher Frederick Nietzsche attempted through his work the establishment of a philosophical brand of therapy for those who found no relief from a world bent on the destruction of individual happiness, and proposed that emotions, "derive from and register our evaluation of our power to shape or control the external world" (Ure, 2009).

IT IS from man's inability to comprehend his inability to shape everything in the outside world that negative emotions spring forth to obstruct happiness, productivity, free thought, and everything else associated with successful, happy individuals. This confusion gives way to despair and the creation of artifices and constructs aimed at creating the illusion of control, such as deification of weather patterns and natural disasters common to virtually all ancient cultures.

BUT TO APPROACH this dilemma with a new perspective on free will, we can begin to unpack how a steadfast will can circumvent the despair described by Nietzsche. After all, we have a will to choose our thoughts, which engenders a will to decide whether or not we grapple with our personal ineffectiveness in the first place. By choosing—an act of free will— to disregard negative circumstances as a cause for alarm, we are effectively choosing to hamper our emotional connection with the situation that is giving rise to the stress reaction.

PUTTING free will in a position of primacy when considering its relation to human emotion gives an individual more agency in determining the outcome of their efforts and hopes because it removes the layer of uncertainty that comes from an overly emotional response. It aids in the keeping of a clear head and the ability to rationally debate about a circumstance and provides the sage with a valuable tool in his arsenal of techniques for bearing the struggles of the modern world in a philosophically virtuous manner.

IMPLEMENTING STOICISM

Stoics through the ages have argued for the uselessness of philosophical inquiry if it did not lead to some measurable change in one's actions or lifestyle. From the original Stoics to revivalists such as Justus Lipsius, Stoic philosophers have long been proponents of supplying their audiences with proscriptive ideas about how to enact their philosophies in the "real world". With the advent of modern Stoicism, this proscriptive effort to provide readerships and scholars with schema for enacting the changes they wish to make has taken the guise of psychological therapies and dialogues addressing the circumstances that surround emotional upheavals.

. . .

FROM THE ORIGINAL MODERN STOIC, Albert Ellis and his Rational Emotive Therapy to other incarnations of cognitive behavioral therapy that mold themselves around the Stoic maxim that negative emotions arise from negative thought, many of the leading scholars publishing today about modern Stoicism agree that depression and negative outlooks are the result of misaligned views of how the world *should be.*

UNFORTUNATELY FOR THOSE suffering from depression as a result of the four frameworks laid out by Ellis, we have no control over how the world should be, no say in its function other than when that function intersects with our own actions and lives. More importantly, even the assertion that the world is or is not as it should be in order to cultivate happiness is based on an incorrect supposition that the world should be any particular way at all.

FOLLOWING from the ancient Stoic thought, we can argue that the world is laid out by providential design, and if we are not able to accept that explanation because of our modernity or our disbelief in higher powers, we still must infer that world is laid out by the machinations of history that extend centuries before our own time. Certainly, this does not imply that humans can do nothing to better themselves or the world, and, in fact, the merger of psychology and philosophy as embodied by modern Stoicism represents an attempt do just that. The methodology is unorthodox: RET and its cognitive behavioral descendants all stem from the stoic notion that certain aspects of the world's functions lie outside our control, and these brands of psychotherapy are all firmly devoted to the notion that to change our thoughts, we must first change our long-held associations and mental congruences.

THIS DOES NOT MEAN that modern Stoicism is incapable of changing the world, only that it does so through indirect channels by seeking to change its adherents' perception of the world.

VARIOUS SCHOLARS of our contemporary times have taken up the flag of Stoicism and advocated for a return to simplicity, an introspective worldview, and high regard for the rule of logic and reason.

Embracing this outlook is beneficial to individuals and societies, and the merger of behavioral oriented therapies with the philosophical teachings of Stoics such as Albert Ellis and Aaron T. Beck and Lawrence Becker is a vehicle for bringing this new frame of thought to the people who need it most: those suffering from anxiety, depression, listlessness, and lethargy.

THE TEACHINGS of modern Stoicism are manifold and diverse, and we will be spending this next chapter discussing some of the current implementations of stoic principles in modern psychology.

WHY BOTHER? The Point of Stoicism

As modern Stoics, we seek to apply our own rational thoughts and tempered emotions to a world that is anything but rational. The efforts can be futile, and they can be exhausting, and for long periods of time, they can be fruitless. But when we succeed in implementing the stoic way of life in our own daily actions we offer the world an example of how to step back and appreciate the complexities of life for what they are: a web of relationships, a series of interconnected circumstances and stimuli that act upon us and ensnare us like spider webs. Only the way of the stoic sage can prepare us for the hectic and frantic trials of the modern world, strengthening our will and freeing us from the emotional entanglements that drag so many into the mire of lost potential.

BEING A STOIC MEANS ACCEPTING FAILURE. Being a stoic means releasing your control, and, more importantly, your *desire* for control. It means that you are willing to look at a chaotic, ill-planned and uncaring universe and smile at the conflagration, grateful for the visual spectacle and the wild ride. Many of the sages of the previous eras have remarked about the sage's inability to get angry, or the sage's steadfast determination in the face of stunning horrors and tragedy. Now more than ever, their teachings of old are becoming a prerequisite for life in a world that seems to only speed up, grow more cluttered, and drive people further apart.

WE HAVE no control over that, though, as we now know. We are on our way to becoming stoics, and the implications of our teachings remind us that the tangled web of the world and its passions are a snare that will tighten around our necks if we allow it and that we have no control over the knot.

WHAT WE DO control is whether or not we stick our necks into it. This is what matters. This is what we must accept if we are to live the way of the Stoic sage, walk in the footprints of Zeno and Epictetus, Marcus Aurelius the Philosopher King and Justus Lipsius. We don't need to fix the world, and we don't need to *fix ourselves*. Both of these things are as they are, preordained or not, deterministic or free. The only thing that we do have power over is the course of thought through our mind and the direction that thought takes. And who knows? Perhaps by setting the example of the Stoic sage, we can enact change in the world, and we can implement the philosophies of Zeno of Citium in a manner that will bring about, if not a perfect world, at least a tempered one, a world in which rationality exercises its will over emotions, and in which we as a society have given up on our lofty expectations of greatness, content rather, to spend our days in contemplation and meditation.

. . .

SO IN ORDER TO reach that level of sagely wisdom, we will breakdown some of the ways in which Stoicism has already been applied, and possibly work toward some modal synergy that will give rise to a unified, coherent definition of what it means to be a sage in the modern era, and how that wisdom can change your life for the better.

LOGOTHERAPY and the Horrors of the Holocaust

Not many people over the course of human history have known the extent of man's inherent evil than philosopher and psychologist Viktor Frankl. An Austrian Jew and psychologist in the first half of the twentieth century, Frankl` witnessed the horrors of four concentration camps and endured decades of subjugation, dehumanization, and despair at the hands of a world power that certainly lied outside his control (Bulka, 1975). In a sense, his story is the quintessential tale of the modern Stoic, a stark reminder of the powers of the mind and the ability to remain cognizant and effective in the face of the most appalling and insurmountable obstacles.

. . .

DURING HIS TIME in the camps, Viktor Frankl developed a philosophical framework that he called logotherapy, which built on the bones of other great Austrian psychotherapists such as Freud, and culminated eventually in the axiom that meaning—not pleasure—is the essential piece of the puzzle for an "existentially viable life" (Bulka, 1975). It is, in other words, the search for meaning which supplies us with meaning. The only problem, according to Frankl's theory, is that for so many of us, for so many years of our seemingly long life, we wallow in meaninglessness. We have no set direction, and the vast expanse of both physical and emotional worlds can seem a terrifying, empty void in the face of the atrocities of mankind. No one knew this more than Viktor Frankl.

BUT FOR FRANKL, just like for Zeno and Epictetus and the Stoics of old, suffering was not inherently bad, for suffering had the capacity to provide meaning in a meaningless world. Suffering bestowed upon the sufferer an opportunity to see the world for what it was and to make amends with that world, rather than railing against it with hopeless, impotent, and obstructive fury.

. . .

HIS THEORY OF LOGOTHERAPY, both as a practical psychology and an intellectual brand of philosophy, gives voice and body to the idea of suffering as an agent of human improvement. In a paradoxical juxtaposition, Frankl argues that this sense of meaninglessness engendered by the trials of the world gives the individual life both agency and a sense of meaning that stems directly from one's method of dealing with that very meaninglessness we all must confront.

IN TRUE STOIC FASHION, logotherapy, as defined by Frankl, is a theory that lauds human guilt as an opportunity for improves, considers the finality of death a mirror through which we can measure our lives, and praises imperfection as the perfect state of humankind. In short, everything about his theory is an embodiment of the original Stoic ethic and framework, enacted in the modern era to confront modern problems, Through Frankl's example, we can begin to analyze our own search for meaning and begin to see through an apathetic lens the manner in which the world acts upon us in ways that seem random, ill-fated, or absurd. He provides us with a framework through which we can actualize our Stoic principles.

DURING HIS CAREER AS A PSYCHOLOGIST, Frankl used the tenets of logotherapy to treat anxiety and depression, obsessive-compulsive disorder, and in some cases even schizophrenia. He believed in his treatment methodologies because he found that all of these conditions—and many more—stem from dysfunction within the sufferer that disallows the individual in question from viewing oneself as an agent. This gets back to the heart of modern Stoicism. To not be an agent is to not be able to act on the world. Those who do not see themselves as agents are passive observers of the world and are burgeoned by the inexhaustible capacity of the larger forces of the world to destroy and crush the wellbeing of the individual.

BY REORIENTING THOUGHT along the lines of logotherapy entails the sufferer's confrontation of the existential vacuum of meaninglessness and come out with an understanding that the "meaning of it all," the purpose of our lives, is to *make* the meaning. To find it within ourselves and use our powers of agency to carve it out of the uncaring void.

HIS OWN LIFE is a paragon of virtue in that it exemplifies the strength of will that is present in all mankind. Just as Epictetus braved the horrors of slavery and came out with a stoic calm and a placid, emotional reserve, just as Seneca the Younger escaped the intrigues of Nero's court with his life and philosophy intact, so too does Viktor Frankl use the horrors of one man against another as a catalyst to the inception of a new philosophical understanding of man as an animal, and a creature driven by desire and want and lust for more.

IN HIS PHILOSOPHY, there is no way that man can totally escape the dragnet of society. There are no solitary figures in solitary existence. There is only the vast conglomeration of man and world, where the horrors that the combination engenders does not need to be frowned upon and fought against, only accepted and used as a tool by which we can measure the effects of the world on our own frame of mind and work to limit that effect as best we can.

EVEN IN SUFFERING, there is meaning, and this, in the end, is the crux of Frankl's philosophy formed in the crucible of Holocaust and the horror of an uncaring world. To remember this lesson is to begin the path of the stoic and to begin that path, one must first accept that we have limited agency at best when we try to act upon the greater world, but we have complete and total agency and supremacy over what we allow into our minds and hearts.

RATIONAL EMOTIVE THERAPY: A Deeper Look

As discussed earlier, Rational Emotive Therapy (RET) is one modern Stoicism's first practical applications developed in the mid-twentieth century by Alfred Ellis to combat the synergy and causal relationship between inherently unstable beliefs and the damaging emotional conflicts that arise from inflated expectation and failure.

. . .

FOR THOSE WITH a sense of inflated expectation about the world and what it should or should offer to the individual, the daily failures that comprise most of our lives is a colossal, terrifying edifice of ineffective thought. We lose ourselves in the sea of misspent energy and the sensation of being lost hampers our ability to make sense of the world and its agents. This is detrimental to our happiness, our success, and our emotional wellbeing and Ellis preaches that by rationalizing these expectations, we can more effectively deal with that which lies outside the realm of our control.

THROUGH RET, we become our own therapists. We become the writer of our own futures and we learn to use the powers of our mind and will to overcome that which previously seemed impossible (Vernon, 1998).

THE SECRETS of RET lie in that it gives the practitioner a sense of power over one's emotions, and teaches them to prevent the emotional situations that give rise to depression from occurring in the first place. The primary tenet the treatment plan is to inculcate individuals with the notion that emotions are really nothing more than functions of thought, and that by changing the thought, we change the emotional response. To its utmost extent, this technique can be used to make the best of any situation and can shed a light of positivity on the direst of circumstances.

MORE IMPORTANTLY, to accept one's thoughts as the catalyst of emotion allows the individual to see one's self in the best light. By rationally analyzing our emotions, we engage in self-acceptance and reap the benefits of the sage who worries not about the pressures exerted by outside forces. These practices place the ball firmly in our own court, so to speak, and gives the student the tools with which to construct a clear division between "performance and worth" (Vernon 1998).

IN OUR SOCIETY, we fail to do this, and we often see a failure to perform as a detriment to our character or a sign of weakness of spirit that represents an inherent flaw in our cognition and belief systems. But this is unnecessary and is symptomatic of the manner in which our societal values are structured around old ideals of individualism and success. It is a paradigm that has been a focal point of American and western culture for the large majority of history and, through the years, has contributed to a society in which the fortunate few can earn great power and wealth at the expense of the unfortunate masses.

WE KNOW, through at Stoic philosophical undertakings, that these are meaningless trappings that were just as incongruent with a happy and virtuous life in Zeno's time as they are in our own. RET harkens back to the original school of thought in that it discounts our performance at any given task as a measure of our validity as human beings. It takes pride in the fact that we are built to fail and built to overcome failure if we practice mindful resilience and a studied disregard for that which is not inherent to our sense of being.

WITHIN RET, as a school of thought, there exists a dichotomy of belief that humans hold, with the dividing line separating those beliefs which are rational from those which aren't. For Ellis, the crux of human emotional fallibility lies in what he calls the "shoulds, musts, and wants" (Vernon, 1998). These fall under the category of irrational beliefs and stand as a deterministic structure preventing people from getting beyond their failures to reach a state of meditative calm. By subjecting ourselves to these irrational beliefs, we limit our ability to inspect our own selves.

WE FAIL to live up to the Greek maxim of knowing thyself because we approach the effort from a rigged standpoint: of course we can't know ourselves when we spend our time hung up on outside forces analyzed through an assumptive mode of thought, holding onto the negativity that engenders depression and inactivity because that very negativity is a façade so vast we cannot see around it. We cannot get to the heart of things when we don't even realize the limitations we face exist outside our selves.

ESSENTIALLY, RET is modern Stoicism's attempt to get across the thought that we are in control. It attempts to delineate where the bounds of that control lie and shift our focus to the arenas in which studied reflection can serve a practical and positive purpose.

THROUGH THE DISPUTATION of irrational belief, Ellis and the modern Stoics believe that humans have the power to control their own emotions by *thinking differently*. This is the central point of view that has remained solidly at the center of Stoic thought throughout the ages and has informed some of the world's most enlightened thinkers. The beauty of this philosophy is that it takes such elevated thought and brings it to the people.

JUST AS ZENO preached on the steps of Athens rather than in Aristotelian schools of privacy reserved for the privileged, Ellis's RET is a tool that we can all use to better ourselves, to take control of our emotions and to finally disengage with our preoccupation with negativity.

STOICISM IN PRACTICE

*H*ow can we use the lessons of modern Stoics? How can RET and logotherapy and their descendants remind us of who we are, and serve as a bastion of calm in the ever-changing sea of despair that the world may seem, at times, to be? These questions have remained central to the philosophical discourse surrounding Stoicism and are truly the main focus of the school of thought going back to antiquity.

In order to put these philosophies into practice, I would like to propose two different courses of action we can take. These courses represent the manner in which (1) we can change our lives for the better through thought exercises, and (2) the manner in which we can change our lives through putting philosophy into physical practice through action in the real world. As the old Stoics proclaimed, philosophy should be an art in practice more than it should be a discourse on sophism (Baltzly, 2018).

IN THIS CHAPTER, we will inspect the philosophical life for any hint as to where we might go from here. Any clues about the direction our self-study should take. We will work on enacting principles and activities that foster positivity, productivity, and most importantly, acceptance of who we are as individuals because, in the end, this is what philosophical inquiry has been about since Socrates first began his dialogues in the centuries before Zeno.

BY PRACTICING PHILOSOPHY, our aim is the betterment of ourselves, and this cannot be accomplished until we acknowledge the problems that we face and their causes. We must stand face to face with the void of a meaningless world and learn from its indifference that if we don't matter to it, it should not matter to us. So much of the strife of the past century is engendered by our inability to see this.

SO MUCH ANGUISH is caused by attempting the impossible without fully recognizing the fact that one endeavor or another might be just that: not possible. To fail in the face of the impossible is only for those who have learned to accept what they cannot change. For all others, the constant inability to carve out a safe place in the world leads to reinforcing feelings of doubt in our own innate abilities. We are here to prove that this does not have to be the way. Humanity need not wallow in her own inabilities when there is so much she is capable of.

How to Use a 2,500 Year Old Philosophy in the Modern World

Obviously, much has changed in the world since Zeno walked the streets of Athens, since Marcus Aurelius sat in wisdom on the throne of a great empire. So many developments are taken as commonplace nowadays that the ancient Stoics would not have been able to conceive of in the most vivid and hallucinogenic imaginings. The apathy of the Industrial Age, where man was quite literally trodden into the mud by the advances of machine technology, and stood as tiny figurines in the shadow of its own creations, the destitution of the World Wars and the genocides that have swept the planet, all of these are emblematic of the suffering forced upon one human from another, and all can be understood as the product of irrational and untampered desired railed against by the ancient Stoics.

MANY OF THE facets of ancient Stoicism no longer apply to the scientific age we live in, such as their views on physics and the natural world. We no longer need to reinforce our beliefs through the objectification of deities, and we don't need to hold original aspects of Stoic virtue as the primal factor in determining a good life. What we do need, and what Stoicism still provides its adherents, is the relative calm state of mind that is enhanced by a Stoic outlook.

THE IDEAL STOIC, as defined by Zeno of Citium and various others, is still a model of behavior that transcends societal and cultural boundaries and can be beneficial to virtually every human living on this planet. This is because we all face strife.

WE ALL SEEK MEANING, and we are all frustrated or confused by that which we cannot rightly confront or understand. These feelings of fear or confusion are as old as mankind itself, but through an embrace of the Stoic mindset, they may be alleviated if we cultivate a sense of understanding of ourselves in relation to the world as a whole. This is was Zeno preached, that we must understand ourselves before seeking to change anything about us or the world we live in. A thought that has echoed through the ages, we see grappling with self-evident in Marcus Aurelius' *Meditations* just as surely as we see it in Justus Lipsius religious identity crises.

BUT THE TRIALS of others can serve to benefit us. By learning about the manner in which many Stoics, both modern and ancient, have handled adversity, we are given a strong series of examples that ratify the original tenets of Stoic thought: an enlightened sage worries only about that which he or she can control. There is no use in foundering in the iniquity

MASTERING THE STOIC WAY OF LIFE

of failure when we can realize that certain tasks are doomed to fail outright. Remembering this provides a valuable tool in the Stoic's armament to get beyond the minutiae of daily life, and gives us a perspective endowed with greater scope in regard to the problems that we face.

Neuroplasticity and Our Changing Brains

One of the primary paradoxes of Stoicism lies in the fact that it holds the outside world to be essentially deterministic and unchanging. From the moment Zeno argued for a providential design of the cosmos, Stoicism was constantly trying to defend the notion that the world cannot be changed. This is juxtaposed by the notion that, unlike the world at large, our brains are not deterministic in nature, and despite what we may have been inculcated with at a young age, we still always possess the capacity for change. In modern psychology, the ability of our brain to change and grow as we accumulate new experiences is called "neuroplasticity" (Summerhays, 2010).

· · ·

APPLYING concepts of neuroplasticity to the Stoic mindset reveals congruencies between the two fields of study. Groundbreaking research into the field of neuroplasticity helped the study of the human mind escape the deterministic views of the Freudians, who held that once damaged, the best a human adult could hope for was to pick up the pieces and put them back together as best they can. As Stoics we hold that the notion of an unchanging brain is far more terrifying than that of an unchanging world, and the advent of adult neuroplasticity has given credence to the teachings of the ancient Greek philosophers by proving, biologically, that we do have power over our own thoughts, and that we can affect change in those patterns if we find them not to our liking.

THIS IDEA HAS BEEN BACKED up scientific research related to the interactions between the different lobes of our frontal cortices, and points the finger at religious practices as one possible activity that has been shown to increase the dominance of one's left frontal cortex, most commonly associated with producing feelings of happiness (Summerhays, 2010).

·   ·   ·

EVEN THE ANCIENT philosophers without the aid of modern medicine were able to figure out that the human spirit is divided, and is, in a sense, constantly at war with itself in determining emotion, action, and thought. But with the advent of brain mapping technology, this has become a documented fact, and the cross conversation of left and right brain activities is believed to be responsible, or at least a strong determining factor in our ability to maintain happiness.

IF THE STOICS ARE CORRECT, and we have control over our own thoughts, and by extension, our emotions, these findings come as a great relief. They imply the validity of some of our most ancient and long-standing beliefs, and they serve as a confidence booster for those who might be experiencing difficulty in rearranging their thought patterns toward a more positive bent. Furthermore, they refute claims of the genetic origins of stress-related conditions and, barring an outright disproval of such notions, provide the scholar and sage with a means to combat the stressors that many perceive to be outside of individual control.

· · ·

NEUROPLASTICITY ALSO CARRIES implications for the long term employment of Stoic values applied to daily life. By arguing that repetition alters one's brain chemistry, this field of study implies by extension that repetition, over time, makes the maintenance of happiness and fortitude in the face of adversity an exponentially more accessible path for those struggling with such issues.

RESEARCH INTO STRESS and traumatic memories in regard to sufferers of PTSD has already turned up positive results in the search to prove the existence and possibility of "function changes due to exposure treatment" (Kolassa and Elbert, 2007). This has vast implications for the implementation of Stoic thought. If exposure to certain stimuli has been clinically proven to enact functional changes in our brain's hardware—if it literally rewires the neurons and receptors to behave differently—then Stoicism emerges again in history as a viable school of thought effective in addressing societal ills such as depression and anxiety.

. . .

NEUROPLASTICITY IS ONLY one advancement in the psychological understanding of the human mind and spirit that has helped to create a strong case for the importance of Stoicism. By mapping the brain and furthering our understanding of its function, we are not necessarily treading new ground or making new discoveries, but rather, we are bolstering our belief in that which has existed in philosophical history for twenty-five hundred years. The mind is malleable, and we now have the technology to prove that fact.

AFFIRMATIONS and the Power of Positivity

Put simply, affirmations are an attempt to force-feed positive thoughts into our brains. They work through repetition and function through the same mechanisms that power ideas of neuroplasticity. It is a time-honored method of reinforcing certain behaviors while discrediting others and has been spoofed widely across the American cultural milieu throughout the past century. Think of Bart Simpson writing on the chalkboard during the opening theme of the hit animated comedy *The Simpsons*. It may seem like a comical example, but it speaks to the degree in which we can change our attitudes—or attempt to—

though the repetition of positive thoughts. It is a practice entered into by public speakers, students, children, and cancer patients in an effort to stem the devastating effect of paranoia, self-doubt, and anxiety (Wood, et al, 2009). Positive statements lift self-esteem, empower the speaker, and instill confidence. By embracing this idea, the Stoic thinker is given another valuable tool for the improvement of one's self.

A MAJOR PSYCHOLOGICAL principle is at work in determining the efficacy of positive self-statement. Reinforcement holds that, as social animals, humans learn from one another and are conditioned to repeat actions that have engendered positive responses in the past. This technique is used in grade schools throughout the nation, but it is still effective when used in adult communities as well.

ACCORDING TO REINFORCEMENT THEORY, Pavlov's proverbial dogs salivate at the sound of a bell because the notion has been reinforced in their mind that the taste of fresh meat will follow that sound. Similarly, children in school are subjected to reinforcement, and the use of this technique in schools has provided evidence that "the use of suggestion involves the programming of positive expectation" (Downing, 1986). Studies have linked affirmations with positive behavior change in children, and given what we know about neuroplasticity, there is nothing to stop them from working on adults as well (Downing, 1986).

THE BEAUTY of affirmations as a tool for self-improvement and the realigning of negative impressions lies in its simplicity. It requires nothing but the will to engage in self-help and is accessible to virtually everybody in the world, spanning cultural differences and age boundaries. Through repetition, neuroplasticity and the use of positive affirmations, we are given a valuable head start on our question for betterment and improvement, and the building blocks of such a task are literally hardwired into us and social being.

THIS, too, should come as a relief to Stoics. Studies related to the efficacy of positive affirmations have been varied in their results, but the notion of their efficacy is entrenched in Stoic thought. Stoics have hammered into the collective conscience for ages the idea that we can change our own perceptions and attitudes by thinking differently. If certain scientists have found evidence claiming otherwise, this should bother us no more than Epictetus' broken leg bothered him. Despite his adversity, he rose up to the challenge and left an indelible mark on the history of human cognition and thought despite the cultural norms saying that he was born into servitude. In the same way, we as Stoics can choose to ignore the unfavorable reviews of affirmation as a psychology technique for betterment.

THIS IDEA IS ALSO TIED up in what we have called a "self-fulfilling prophecy." Simply put, these "prophecies" are nothing more than a system of thought that reinforces itself through repetition. In true Stoic form, we can recognize self-fulfilling prophecy as indifferent, neither good nor bad, because thinking in that mode does not necessitate a mental or happiness or despondency. Self-fulfilling prophecies simply represent a method of thinking that is common among humans and points to the effectiveness of neuroplasticity and repetition in determining attitudes and outlooks.

. . .

A THOUGHT PATTERN can be considered a self-fulfilling prophecy when it is both recurring and self-reinforcing. Thinking that "I will fail," is not the same thing as thinking "I will fail *because I always fail.*" The former is merely a negative thought, but when it is amended as it is in the latter statement, it becomes a self-fulfilling prophecy. This is because that by stating "I will fail because I always fail," the speaker is affirming that the failure is predetermined and originates from the speaker's very nature as a failure. It becomes nearly impossible to succeed at a task with such an attitude, and the repeated failures stacked on top of one another create a slippery slope that is hard to climb off of. After all, it is hard to discount the logic in such a statement when confronted by the vast empirical evidence of numerous failures, one after the other.

BUT TO BREAK THAT MOLD, we don't need to combat self-fulfilling prophecies, we simply need to reorient them so that their inherent meanings are more in line with positive thought and self-confidence. Affirmations are nothing more than self-fulfilling prophecy in this way. In theory, just as the person who claims failure because that has always been the case will likely fail, the person who claims the opposite is more likely to succeed. Given the exponential nature of this type of self-statement, either the benefits or the negative consequences will compound.

FOR THIS REASON, affirmations represent a dangerous line, but by walking that line and proving our fortitude to ourselves, we come out on the other side with a great tool used to battle inefficiency, laziness, poor performance, and many other ill-conceived factors of life that contribute to our dissolving wellbeing.

AFFIRMATIONS REMIND us consciously of the person we want to be at the same time they alter the person we are in ways that are far less tangible. By keeping our goals and our self-esteem in mind through the art of affirmation, we start to improve our attitudes simply by stating an attitude improvement to be the case. It is because of this dual nature of the helpfulness of affirmations that they must be listed among the veritable mind training activities that the Stoic must employ to lead the life of a sage.

STOICISM IN ACTION

hus far we have analyzed the philosophical tenets of the Stoic move-ment, traced its history through antiquity, into the Enlightenment and up to the modern-day, paying attention to its evolution as a practical philosophy that seeks to escape the classroom and break free into the world of daily life, and inspected some of the science that reveal the neurology of the Stoic's mind. In this final chapter, we will discuss daily practices that can lead to real and measurable improvements in life, task management, and self-confidence. These are simple practices, but that does not take away from the great powers of improve-ment that they bestow upon the studied sage.

. . .

FROM THE EASE of affirmation or simple schedule keeping, we begin to see the rise of a new identity from within people who have previously struggled to hold up under the pressures of modern life. Building blocks compile, and after a short while, the fledgling Stoic is capable of handling stress, facing the meaningless void and finding meaning within, and meeting a valid and reasonable expectation for success that is held not only by ourselves but by our peers as well. Stoic mindfulness is a psychology technique modeled on the cognitive behavioral therapy technique listed above, with the simple aim of helping suffering individuals regain control of their lives.

CONFIDENCE BUILDING EXERCISES, accurate planning, and self-evaluation are critical to success in the reordering of one's mind, and here, we will get into the nuts and bolts of what will be required.

SCHEDULING: A Necessary Evil

Nobody likes living by a schedule. If given our own way, we would be free to pursue whatever ventures we felt were beneficial to us in our own time. But unfortunately, we live in a communal society built on interpersonal relationships. Our brains are hardwired for this type of socially-oriented behavior and it can be hard to feel like we are living a full life without partaking in the society around us. Doing so comes with its ups and downs, and the requirement of maintaining schedules is arguably one of the downs. Considering its necessity, however, will shed light on time management skills that allow us to be more prepared when adversity does strike. Keeping to a schedule allows you greater control of your day, your week, your month, and keeps the achievement of relevant goals on schedule.

IN THIS WAY, keeping a schedule can actually serve as something of a confidence booster. Everybody loves to cross things off their to-do lists, and the physical manifestation of success, embodied by that singular action brings forth an air of achievement and contributes to a feeling of *getting things done.* So why not turn your entire schedule into one long to-do list? Doing so will not only keep you on track but will also improve your mood as you watch the pile of accomplishments to set out upon dwindle.

. . .

SINCE TIME IS a natural part of humankind's perception of the world, it is just as inescapable as the natural disasters that railed Ancient Greece. If that is so, the Stoic has no need to worry about its flow because there is nothing to be done about its passage. We are simply along for the ride and have an allotted amount of time with which to foster a well-lived life. That being the case, it seems foolish to waste time, and the Stoic would argue that, even if you can't alter its passage, you do have control over how it's spent. Nothing feels worse than a day wasted, and nothing can be more detrimental to one's mental state than the feeling of opportunities gone by or chances missed.

TIME MANAGEMENT AIDS in all of this, and by keeping your activities squarely planned, you increase your chances at attaining happiness because you decrease the amount of time you spend agonizing over the second hand as it ticks away the minutes until your deadline, or your speech, or your advertising pitch.

. . .

ANDREAS ATHANAS

PLANNING KEEPS you proactive and prevents stress from accumulating. If the ethos of the Stoic philosophy is one of philosophy in action rather than philosophy in argument then there can be no better homage to our ancient predecessors than to ensure you remain active and participatory in your own quest for improvement.

VALUE INTROSPECTION

Values and what we hold dear forms a major component of Stoic philosophy. Epictetus informs us that even though we are born with the preconceived notion that that which is good is worthy of "unconditional pursuit" (Graver 2017). He also writes that the error mankind has made lies in that this notion of the good is applied in the wrong direction. This, for the Stoic, is a problem of value systems, and the alignment of such with external factors promising the false illusion of happiness.

TO BE a true Stoic sage is to value only that which lies within the control of your own willpower. Attaching significant value to anything outside of oneself leads to inevitable disillusion when that valued object or principle is altered by the world or proves to be an unhealthy influence.

BECAUSE OF THIS, the Stoic must practice value introspection by constantly meditating on their values and ensuring that they are living up to the values that are inherent to themselves. To mold our thoughts into the framework of Epictetus' philosophical claims, we would need to recognize external phenomena that have deterministic powers over our state of being might be indifferent according to classical Stoic philosophy, because taken of themselves, these external phenomena neither guarantee nor inhibit a true state of virtuous happiness. But we also need to recognize that how we handle these externals—as they are dubbed by Epictetus himself—is not indifferent. This handling of the external world is either good or bad, depending on how well it equates to the pursuit of happiness.

IN TERMS OF VALUE INTROSPECTION, it is important to consider the effects of that which we pursue on our state of mind. Certainly, some pursuits are innate to our being biological creatures. Desires for food, sex, and shelter are natural, and in the modern world there can be very few arguments made against their pursuit, but how well does this notion translate over other fields of life? The more complex the world becomes, the more we are bombarded by new lists of this to pursue—be they intellectual pursuits, spiritual pursuits or material pursuits—and it is up to us to take a step back from the ebb and flow of daily life to evaluate whether or not that which we pursue is inherently good for our wellbeing.

THIS MIGHT SEEM close to the order of common sense, and in some ways, it is. This does not mean that value introspection and necessary adjustments shouldn't be deeply considered by the Stoic sage. After all, from our last section, we discussed the dangers of time wasted. How great is that danger multiplied when we waste time in the pursuit of that which is ultimately damaging to our wellbeing in the first place? Such realizations can be devastating, particularly when they come too late to affect any sort of change, when the damage of the pursuit has already been done.

· · ·

BY REGULARLY REGARDING that which we value as important to us, we can begin to eliminate activities and thought patterns that no longer suit our wellbeing. We can adapt to changing environments as the world around us continues to constantly shift and alter itself. Most importantly, by keeping our value systems in check we can spend time thinking about ourselves, getting to know ourselves, and learning about our own attributes and the unique aspects of our mental framework that make us individuals.

AS MENTIONED EARLIER, the Stoics placed a great deal of import in the value systems that people adhere to. These systems of belief help to shape our personal identities and our happiness and fulfillment in life is derivative to maintain a system of values that is reasonably enough in line with greater society so as not to impede human interaction, but also unique to our own personalities and mindsets. Frequent introspection and meditation, in this regard, help to ensure that we live a fulfilling, prosperous and rich life by forcing us to reckon with ourselves in an evaluative, nonjudgmental manner. This is essential for a life well-lived because without introspection, we would be lost in our minds, with no way of knowing whether or not we have strayed from the path of the sage until it is too late.

Reevaluating Our Reactions

Our reactions to given stimuli is a direct bearing on our personality, our agency, and our ability to cope with stress. This is a key tenet of Stoic philosophy and daily practice in this field will aid the sage in achieving lasting, meaningful happiness. But how should we go about accomplishing this? To what standards should we hold ourselves?

By keeping track of our emotional reactions, we enable a greater understanding of our personae. We learn what sets us off, what we need to work on, and also how we have improved in our ability to maintain a stoic calm in the face of adversity. This is crucial data for people seeking to better themselves in the face of an uncaring world. We need this information to gauge our true mind state and to come to terms with the areas of mental cognition we seek to improve. Evaluation is a major facet of many philosophies and is called for in practice across many of the world's major religions. This might be because evaluation is the one tool that we have to analyze our own lives. It is the hallmark of the enlightened individual.

IN ORDER TO evaluate your emotional responses to adversity, take note of what ticks you off, what angers you, when you feel depressed or anxious. Try to come to an understanding of what is causing such feelings by thinking within the Stoic framework of what is changeable and unchangeable, what we have agency over, and what is out of our control. It is not enough to sit in traffic angrily, stating to yourself the obvious: I am angry because I am in traffic.

THIS DOES NOT EVEN SCRATCH the surface of why you are angry, and maintaining thoughts such as that strips you of the agency to determine your own life. You are angry because you are in traffic. That notion is possessed of such simplicity that it reduces you—a thinking, breathing, rational human being—to an inanimate object upon which the world can act.

· · ·

IT IS MORE constructive to think along the lines of what actually causes the anger to well *from within*, and to address that issue before you shake your fists or pound your steering wheel in a rage. Whatever the cause may be—you are angrily sitting in traffic because you did not allow yourself enough time to get ready—you must make sure that you don't blame your internal emotions on external factors because the Stoics hold that this is a lie.

EMOTIONS ARE SOLELY SEATED within your heart and mind, within your human spirit. In this amendment to the reason you internalize the cause of your emotions, thereby taking it out of the realm of things over which you have no control, and placing it firmly within your abilities to overcome. If you are angry because you are late and sitting in traffic, just that realization alone is enough to give you a good start. You can temper this angry emotion by ensuring that you don't set yourself up for failure.

EVALUATIVE THOUGHT in regard to human emotion does a great deal of work in helping us understand the causal relationship between stimulus and reaction. It also is a great way for the sage to get to know themselves, providing a great internal forum for deliberation on the traits and attributes that define the sage's personality and identity. Through this practice, we are given the opportunity to make links between the circumstances that create adversity and the manner in which we handle not only the situation but the adversity itself. There is a different way of handling confrontation for every person living on Earth, and by understanding the way in which *you* deal with such strife, you open a door of insight into your own mind that would have otherwise remained closed off to the world philosophic thought.

STOIC PRINCIPLES

THE GREAT INHERITANCE

The ideas put forth by Stoicism are practical, healthy and freeing. Modern Stoicism can anaesthetise unnecessary suffering while helping you push towards a prosperous life.

HISTORIES STOIC PRINCIPLES have been refined over and over again. A process of elimination has occurred over thousands of years, even before we had a name for stoicism and we get to take advantage of the disciplines acted out and recorded for our own benefit.

. . .

WE CAN CHOOSE to live like a Marcus Aurelius or a Seneca by choice.

YOU WILL NEED TO PRACTISE, train and embody the principles set before you.

NO MATTER THE situation you find yourself in, you can choose to be the type of person you want to be.

Natural Process

MOTHER NATURE in all her majestic beauty is going to inflict illness, death and destruction on everything you have ever loved, opening a path for the next generation to take part in this process we call life.

ACCEPTANCE of your own death and the death of everyone you have ever seen helps prepare you for the terrible days of your future.

. . .

THIS GIVES you the chance to be strong when others are weak, comfort the others, prepare arrangements, lift spirits, and be the person your family and friends need you to be. Especially in times of great difficulty loss and struggle.

THE ACCEPTANCE of life processes can free you from excessive fears and living in an overly conservative manner. This acceptance can help when it is necessary for you to take calculated risks so you can advance in your life.

YOU MUST ACCEPT natural processes as your reality.

THE SANDS of time never stops for any of us.

DON'T TIP toe towards your grave, take some calculated chances and prepare for your future.

GRATITUDE VS WANTING

. . .

CHOOSE your thought wisely and control them before they start to control you.

LUCKILY YOUR MIND can only hold so many thought's at a time, this gives you a tremendous power over how you use your mind.

IF YOU TURN off the automatic thoughts and intentionally choose what to think about, you can live a much better experience than letting your brain go into automatic mode. Automatic unconstrained thinking can lead to excessive negative thoughts if you don't take back control. It is necessary to become the person at the wheel and directing where the next thought is going and stopping it in its tracks before it becomes excessive and possibly deluded.

YOU CAN CHOOSE to think of all the things you have in your life and the things you're grateful for or you can concentrate on what you don't have. The second option will lead to the pain of wanting, the pain of thinking things should not be like this.

. . .

IT'S irrational to concentrate on what you don't have until it makes you miserable and destroys your mental health.

THINK about all the things you are grateful for and you will feel better about life.

IF YOU REPEATEDLY CONCENTRATE ON what you don't have, it can take you to some very dark places.

YOUR IMAGINATION, memory and perspective can be your friend or your enemy, separating you from the gifts of life or marching you towards a better one.

THE BUDDHISTS SAY "Free yourself from need and want". This makes me feel better every time I say it but its not the right thing to do for the long term.

HUMANITY WOULD HAVE FADED to dust if we all adopted this philosophy.

. . .

THE EXPECTATION of your wants coming into reality is what can really hurt, expecting all of our endeavours to pay off in the future despite that not being a very realistic outlook is a tope of delusion.

A MORE STOIC view would be to have hopes without expectation, to endure and take action without expecting the end result to look exactly like the picture in your mind.

THE RESULTS of your life will likely be better or worse than you expected and that's ok, as long as you tried your best and gave it everything you had. Turn your mind towards gratitude and feel better or the pain of wanting will destroy the bliss you can feel about the blessings you already have.

REASON

THE STOIC IS like a scientist looking out at the World asking questions, trying things, succeeding and failing.

. . .

NOT JUDGING the findings of these trials, documenting and taking mental note of the results.

THE FACTS of life are delivered by mass experimentation.

THE QUALITY of an experiment could be judged by the percentage of variables per experiment.

THE BEST EXPERIMENTS would be performed in massive numbers and address 100% of the variables.

EVEN THEN THERE is still a possibility of error but its the best we have.

THERE ARE many flawed studies and polls but this is to be expected, just because something is not absolutely perfect does not mean we should deem it not valuable.

. . .

SOCIAL STUDIES ARE USUALLY the most difficult to prove as they can have thousands of variables not accounted for. Lying is just one of the variables that can mess with social studies and I imagine it's a large factor in poor quality information.

WE SHOULD NEVER BE SWAYED by one of events, this is what is commonly referred to as anecdotal evidence and should only be part of a discovery and questioning phase of what the true nature of reality is.

YOU MIGHT HAVE to act on something when you only have partial knowledge, this is ok if you cannot find anymore information. Just know that you cannot see the path in front of you as clearly as you might suspect.

TO BE a person of reason you must seek knowledge in any way you can, this way you can find the clearest path towards your goal and avoid the time loss and other pitfalls laid before you.

. . .

QUESTION EVERYTHING you learn and don't come to the position of having a perfectly formulated conclusions. This is the conclusion bias and it stops you receiving new and possibly important information.

TO BE A PERSON OF REASON, you must evaluate information without bias and emotion without your old stories getting in the way of how things are and not just the way you want them to be.

OUR FEELINGS SHOULD NOT CHANGE how we interpret our findings.

THE COGNITIVE BIASES of liking and disliking are probably the strongest forces that can make us dismiss the facts and figures we are presented with.

BEING people of reason means we acknowledge uncomfortable truths , reject group think and don't just take the word of anyone, wether it be from the tongue of an authority, expert, commoner, academic or someone in your family. We look at the facts ourselves and let the facts inform us.

TRY to overcome your cognitive biases and take the opinions of others to be just that, opinions. You have to think for yourself.

CONSTANTLY BE LOOKING for better information, reassess and remake the game plan for any goal you have. Keep experimenting with your life until you find a way that works for you.

SELF RESTRAINT

WHY IS MAKING boundaries good for you?

WE SET boundaries for our children, give up on most teenagers and rarely create new boundaries for ourselves. Most adults rarely ever make new boundaries for themselves.

· · ·

THE ONLY ADULT boundaries we see with any regularity are diet and alcohol related which is great, as you need to protect your body.

WHAT ABOUT SETTING boundaries for your mind and emotions. The destructive emotions and thought patterns need to be reigned in, emotions like jealousy and anger can destroy your life if they are not controlled.

EVEN POSITIVE EMOTIONS like lust can have negative effects, without the use of self control, you can lose your family in a moment of passion.

THIS IS why you must train yourself to stop your emotional excesses.

SOMETIMES THINGS ARE DIFFICULT, it is like you don't have emotions, the emotions have you. You become a slave to the warm rush of chemicals rushing through your veins, you are no longer rational, you are like a junkie out of your mind on the natural highs of your bodies chemistry.

MANY PEOPLE BECOME addicted to extreme emotions, they look for drama where it doesn't exist, they create their next fix any way they can, they are drunks without a bottle.

YOU DON'T HAVE to become a victim of your emotions, you can slow yourself down and become the observer of these chemical reactions.

FEEL the emotions and watch how they start to cloud your thinking, maintain control so you don't become the automaton of the emotions, a barely recognisable sub personality that will destroy its own life in order to express the peak of the emotional state.

TAKE control of your mental and physical excesses before they decrease the quality of your life.

· · ·

METTLE

SOME PEOPLE THINK that Stoicism is all about grit and determination, there is some truth to this but its not for the reasons everyone assumes.

THE OUTSIDE OBSERVER of the Stoics would think that it's a conscious effort to use grit and determination to get things done.

I BELIEVE that grit and determination are not part of the equation, it just looks that way, grit and determination are just a buy product of a rational philosophy on life.

THE DIFFICULTY in the pursuit of anything you want should become irrelevant once you have made the decision to do it. External factors that cause physical and psychological pain should already be factored into your plan, any road block is now just part of the process.

· · ·

YOU HAVE DECIDED on the price you are willing to pay to get the things you want, time, sweat, disappointment, discomfort and all sorts of sacrifices might have to be endured to get to your destination. If you are willing to pay with everything you have except disability and death you will have a very good chance to get where you want to go.

YOU MIGHT LOSE years or decades in this pursuit, you might lose friends and family who are not supportive, you might have to let go of other wishes you had for your life, but what's the alternative? You are going to pass the years anyway, bad friends will eventually lose touch with you and you can't have everything.

I HOPE you see now that it is irrational to not go for the things you want. It might take a lifelong struggle to get there, that will probably look like grit to most people. The truth is what looks like grit is simply just the opposite of defeat, you haven't given in and given up on living.

. . .

METTLE, grit, determination is just the efforts necessary to attain a worthy cause.

THE SPEECH CHURCHILL delivered to convince parliament we need to go to war with the Nazis makes the previously mentioned points.

"WE BEFORE US have an ordeal of the most grievous kind.

We before us have many long months of struggle and suffering.

You ask, what is our policy?

I can say: It is to wage war, by sea, land and air, with all our might and all the strength that god can give us;

To wage war against a monstrous tyranny, never surpassed in the dark lamentable catalogue of human crime.

That is our policy.

You ask, what is our aim? I can answer in one word: It is victory, victory at all costs, victory in spite of all terror, victory however long and hard the road may be;

For without victory, there is no survival.

Let that be realised;

No survival for the British Empire, no survival for all that the British Empire stood for, no survival of the urge and impulse of the ages, that mankind will move forwards towards its goal.

But I take up my task with buoyancy and hope.

I feel sure that our cause will not be suffered to fail among men.

At this time I feel entitled to claim the aid of all, and I say, come then let us go forward together with our united strength."

Live **Your Philosophy**

Be the change or don't speak it, Stoicism is not an intellectual exercise, it is not meant to be a flashy way of thinking or a way to impress others with pretentious ideas.

Its not meant for the armchair philosopher to ponder and recite, its meant for real life situations, at times it seems cold and calculated, that's because nature doesn't care about your zen, you can't meditate your way out of a famine. Life is hard at times and will require you to be strong in times of difficulty.

STOICISM IS A WAY OF BEING, meant for practical real world application, a person trying to control their mind, grounded in reality, working towards things that must be done, in the pursuit of protecting, maintaining and improving their circumstances.

EGO and the stories you hold onto about yourself can distort your reality and detach you from the real world.

LET GO of the merry go round in your mind come back to the present, be the person you want to be, someone that you would admire.

BECOME like the farmer planting seeds for the future, not the person lost in fantasy and story.

. . .

YOU CANNOT plough a field in your mind, you can't learn how to swim by reading a book and you can't live a great life being someone you don't respect.

APPLY a realist view of the World, act more stoically in the face of life and become the person you know you're meant to be, embody the virtuous and courageous parts of yourself and carry them with you.

BE ADMIRABLE FOR YOURSELF.

PRUDENCE

THINKING AHEAD OF TIME, planning and preparing for a future that is coming no matter how certain we are of the outcome, this is prudence.

SOME SAY that an idiot with a plan can beat a genius without one. I doubt this is true in most cases, but it is obvious to see that someone with a plan has more chance of winning than someone without one.

. . .

A PRUDENT PERSON could just be called a planner, something everyone needs to be to some extent.

BEING steps ahead in any process is a massive advantage, not just in competitive situations like chess and war, everyday situations like cooking and driving to your destination. A cook who prepares all ingredients and has timers set before starting to cook is going to have an easy job just like the driver who has a sat nav, map and mental picture of where he is going.

PREPARATION MAKES LIFE EASIER, makes winning easier it even makes failure easier.

BUILDING IN SYSTEMS for failure within any process helps you keep going even when things are going wrong. It's the spare tyre, puncture kit, emergency assistance and a bike on the roof that saves you being stranded, and this principle should be used in the majority of life's endeavours.

. . .

BEING prudent saves you the time worry and stress of putting out fires constantly throughout your daily life.

IF YOU THINK AHEAD, your mind has space for other necessary thoughts needed in the moment. Catching up is much harder than starting close to the finish line, so think ahead.

Realism

FANTASY VERSUS REALITY, an invisible war for your mind.

ART TRIES to mimic life and life tries to mimic art, both do a bad job.

SHAKESPEARE SAID "We are all actors and the World is our stage"

. . .

EVEN WORSE THAN this partial truth is the way our own personalities are warped by popular media and other influences.

HOW EMBARRASSING TO FIND OUT YOUR role models don't exist in the real World, and the actors who play them display none of their characters virtue.

HAVE fictional characters influenced your personality, voice, walk, cadence and the way you react to life?

THE WAY you act should not be influenced by movies, media, articles and social media because it does not match with reality.

EVEN RECORDED history has been manipulated, we only get to know the things our ancestors wanted us to know. Unfortunately history is written by the victors, and the losers story is usually wiped from the records. The truth of histories stories are more complicated, messy and way less glamorous than we would like to imagine.

OUR ANCESTORS LIVES REALLY HAVE nothing to do with us, so don't identify with the dead, you have nothing to do with them. Even your parents lives are their own and although they impacted you, it does not have to define you in anyway at all. The labels we attribute to ourselves don't really help, they just put you in a box that does not exist. Labelling yourself is like stereotyping yourself into a character that you play, rather than letting yourself just be unique.

SOME PEOPLE ARE PLAYING out stereotypes they have seen portrayed in movies and music to the point of losing their individuality.

EVEN THE SUFFERING of other people is dramatised so you feel like you are the one living a great life wherever you are and you should feel bad for people in worse situations. The truth is, some of the happiest people live in terrible situations it's great if you can help these people but don't think they are any different to you, we all have disaster coming to us eventually. Is a rich man who gets a cancer diagnosis better off than a child living in the Amazon rainforest? We should help the people who cannot help themselves, but we should not feel any different to them, we are all part of the same process of being born trying to live the best we can and then passing away. Everyone suffers and the particular suffering you experience is not unique to you or the group of people you think you belong to, it's just life.

THE FANTASY of the special sufferer is just a fantasy, everyone loses friends and family throughout their life, loses their looks, health and eventually their life. This is the way things are, an unfortunate reality that you don't have to feel guilty about, it's just the way of things.

EVEN THE BEST parts of us can be distorted, even your goals and dreams can be influenced to a direction you don't even really care about. Do you really want to live the life sold to you by tabloid magazines, movies, music, online video and other influencers?

ARE those shallow outcomes the advertisers sell you really going to make you happy? Will it make you fulfilled? or will you find another mountain to climb where you don't enjoy the journey to the top? It makes no sense to find no satisfaction daily while climbing a mountain to someone else's fantasy. Your dreams and goals should be as unique as you are, and your way to get those dreams should be fulfilling or enjoyable as well. Don't climb someone else's mountain based on a tv fantasy of success, you have to live your own path to be successful not someone else's.

ANOTHER FANTASY TO be wary of is the group think delusion, to believe a group has all the answers at all times is just tribalism, it's picking a team and hoping you come out the winner. What are the chances that a free thinkers ideas will line up completely with a groups views? One in a million maybe, and yet so many choose to go along with a groups ideas, following the leaders to the march of their drum. Even when the groups ideas change they stay with their team following the personal development of their leaders and not their own minds. If you don't think for yourself you will never be free and you won't just live with your own delusions but the delusions of the tribe as well.

TRY to rid yourself of the fantasies of identity, stereotype, labels, groups, culture, race, media narratives, Hollywood biases, and every other story about the world, leave as much of your negative past behind you, stop fantasising about struggle, most of the wars we fight are in our heads and will never come to pass.

LET all of the fantasy go, let it burn off and let all of the weight fall from your shoulders, you don't need to carry the narratives of the world and burden yourself with your personal history and the history of the others, only the present and future will ever exist. Try your best to stay in reality or your life will pass you by.

SERENITY PRAYER

*T*he prayer written by Reinhold Neibuhr a Christian theologian sums up a lot of Stoic philosophy.

GOD GRANT me the serenity to accept the things I cannot change; Courage to change the things I can; And the wisdom to know the difference.

LIVING ONE DAY AT A TIME; Enjoying one moment at a time; Accepting hardships as the pathway to peace; Taking, as he did, this sinful World.

· · ·

As it is, not as I would have it; Trusting he will make all things right if I will surrender to his will; So that I may be reasonably happy in this life.

And supremely happy with him forever and ever in the next.

Amen

AFTERWORD

Stoicism has a long and storied history, and the lives of its proponents had enormous influence over shaping its philosophical tenets.

From issues of slavery and freedom to the positioning of man in a religious world, the issues that Stoicism tackled were at the center of the world in which it developed, and the major players in its dissemination spoke of personal events in their lives as a means of providing meaning to the general populace.

Because of its focus on personal issues, it has been a philosophy that humanity has returned to again and again, finding new meaning in the original teachings as society changed and evolved. It served as a groundbreaking innovation in the ancient world in that it called for action in philosophy, rather than existing in the old form of passive discussions about philosophical maxims and principles and obtuse laws that provided no social context for the betterment of the people, and directed people to look within themselves for answers rather than toward the heavens, or the sea, or toward any other manifestation of the unknown.

Instead of directing its energy toward such unknowable facets of life on this planet, Stoicism sought to shed light on the unknown and unexplored depths of the human soul, and because of this focus, it succeeded in capturing the hearts of countless individuals. It became an accessible mode of thought, and the Painted Stoa from which it originally sprang forth saw rejuvenation throughout the ages as various philosophers continued to work within Zeno's framework.

Following in Zeno of Citium's footsteps, these subsequent philosophers have amended and added to that original doctrine of philosophy, proving that the discourse exists as an adaptable model of mental cognition that has been studied for over two millennia. Just as the original Stoics modelled their philosophy on the times in which they lived, seeking to provide their culture with active principles for human enlightenment, the philosophers of Ancient Rome and of the European Middle Ages and the American twentieth century who worked within this field of study also elaborated on the tenets of the philosophy in a manner that was befitting to their cultural norms and the societies they sought to benefit.

With the most recent revival of Stoic thought, we see again how this philosophy has proven to be an ever-changing way of thinking and living that can be molded to the times and the culture of its practitioners. Advancements in sociological and psychological studies inform the new brand of Stoicism, and within its teachings, modern scholars are given the tools they need to thrive in this world, not that of Ancient Greece.

So much of Ancient philosophy is pertinent only to the society from which it springs, but because of the timelessness of its tenets, Stoicism has succeeded where other modes of philosophy from the same time period have fallen by the wayside.

Why is this? What makes the virtue ethics and a naturalistic worldview so compelling to humankind throughout the ages? There are many answers to that question, but I would like to posit that the endearing qualities of Stoicism have lasted for so long in human thought because of the way in which they address not societal problems or global issues, but more humble issues related to self-confidence, agency, and free will. These issues have been a well spring of philosophical insight and many scholars have contributed to our general understanding of their role in human intellectual discussion, but the Stoic interpretations of these issues are possessed of such timelessness because it represents universal attitudes that can be applied in cross-cultural settings.

The primacy of this philosophy and its many incarnations over the ages lies in how it handles human emotions. So many other discourses detract from our control over the emotional forces that rage within us that to hear another view, to find solace in the fact that we *do* control how we feel about the world around us—even if we don't control that world—is a refreshing viewpoint. Perhaps this control of our own emotions is what drove Justus Lipsius to adopt the Stoic mindset in the midst of his exegesis. Perhaps this allowed him to stand before a world that sat on the verge of tearing itself apart over sectarian religious arguments and demand for himself the right to at least determine the flow of his own thoughts and feelings.

The same attitude is taken by modern-day psycho-philosophers who wish to join the two disciplines into one constructive school of thought. Before the dawn of cognitive behavioral therapy and its more Stoic antecedents, psychology was dominated by theories that did away with human agency and heaped upon us only the despair of the past, which could never be changed. The despair engendered by psychological perspectives that rob people of the ability to change their fate gave rise to an interest in a different way of thinking and led modern pioneers of the new Stoicism such as Albert Ellis to question the Freudian paradigms that dominated psychology in the mid-twentieth century. Through searching for a more humanistic approach to psychological disorders, we have once come to the position first proposed by Cleanthes and Chrysippus and Zeno: that the domain of your control extends only so far that which springs forth from your own mind, and the rest is not worth fretting over.

There is a sense of freedom that permeates Stoic thought. Though detractors of the philosophy have lambasted the notion that there might be solace in releasing control, for the Stoic, the recognition of the fact that one cannot control the outside world grants the freedom to focus on the world inside. As a therapeutic practice, modern incarnations of Stoicism have continued the old traditions of self-reflection by imploring individuals to take charge of their own emotions and regulate their reactions to outside stimuli. This is the manner in which the Stoics have decided to approach the problems of societal indifference to the suffering of others, the constancy of war and plague, the ravages of natural disasters. They argue that by fretting over such circumstances, the unenlightened, untampered thinker does nothing to alleviate the problem and only works himself into a frenzy of ill-informed emotions that serve to prevent any sort of higher-order thinking.

It may be extremely difficult to follow the teachings of Zeno, and historians report that he was somewhat of a bitter man, with no family or children. But what Zeno of Citium did have was a firm grasp what he should and shouldn't worry about, and, despite outward appearances of unhappiness, he possessed the qualities of the learned sage, wrangling with emotional uncertainty in a historical period that rested on a precipice, alternately gravitating toward peace or outright desolation.

While it may be difficult to uphold these teachings, the reward for the honorable sage is the happiness of knowing that you are in control of that which comes from within. The world may beat you down, send you torment after torment until you cannot think of anything to do besides cry to the heavens in anguish, but to remember the teachings of Stoicism is to forget about the momentary strife of a world that does not care.

To remember the teachings of Stoicism is to retake control of one's own destiny and stand up to the adversity of the modern world, to find solace in self-reflection, and to master the internal turmoil of a troubled soul, regardless of the situation in the outside world.

This is the gift that Zeno of Citium left to mankind. To follow his path is to honor the life's work of one of the world's greatest thinkers.

REVIEW

To Leave an honest review please use the link below.
http://www.amazon.com/review/create-review?
&asin=B081XCKX4M

I can't express how much we appreciate getting feedback and reviews. They really help to keep the book alive. Thank You so much for reading.

- Andreas Athanas

Bibliography

Baltzly, D. (2019). Stoicism. The Stanford Encyclopedia of Philosophy

Blau, S. (1993). COGNITIVE DARWINISM: Rational-Emotive Therapy and the Theory of Neuronal Group Selection. ETC: A Review of General Semantics, 50(4), 403-441.

Bulka, R. (1975). LOGOTHERAPY AS A RESPONSE TO THE HOLOCAUST. Tradition: A Journal of Orthodox Jewish Thought,15(1/2), 89-96.

Downing, C. (1986). Affirmations: Steps to counter negative, self-fulfilling prophecies. Elementary School Guidance & Counseling,20(3), 174-179. Retrieved from http://www.jstor.org/stable/42868729

Ellis, A. (1975). Rational-Emotive Therapy and the School Counselor. The School Counselor, 22(4), 236-242.

Erskine, A. (2000). Zeno and the Beginning of Stoicism. Classics Ireland, 7, 51-60.

Grant, F. (1915). St. Paul and Stoicism. The Biblical World, 45(5), 268-281.

Graver, M. (2017). Epictetus. The Stanford Encyclopedia of Philosophy

Kamtekar, R. (2018) Marcus Aurelius: The Stanford Encyclopedia of Philosophy

Kolassa, I., & Elbert, T. (2007). Structural and Functional Neuroplasticity in Relation to Traumatic Stress. Current Directions in Psychological Science, 16(6), 321-325.

Mark, J. (2015, February 11). Zeno of Citium. Retrieved from https://www.ancient.eu/Zeno_of_Citium/

Noyen, P. (1955). Marcus Aurelius: The Greatest Practitioner of Stoicism.

Papy, J. (2019), Justus Lipsius. The Stanford Encyclopedia of Philosophy

Summerhays, J. (2010). Twisted Thoughts and Elastic Molecules: Recent Developments in Neuroplasticity. Brigham Young University Studies, 49(1), 160-166.

Ure, M. (2009). Nietzsche's Free Spirit Trilogy and Stoic Therapy. Journal of Nietzsche Studies, (38), 60-84.

Vernon, A. (1998). Promoting Prevention: Applications of Rational Emotive Behavior Therapy. Beyond Behavior, 9(2), 14-24.

Vogt, K. (2016). Seneca. The Stanford Encyclopedia of Philosophy

Printed in the USA
CPSIA information can be obtained
at www.ICGtesting.com
LVHW012250020823
754226LV00026B/706